Mindful Solidarity
A Secular Buddhist Democratic Socialist Dialogue

Praise for *Mindful Solidarity*

A brilliant and accessible analysis of Buddhism and Marxism that weaves together ideas and practices from two seemingly incongruous traditions to reveal a higher synthesis in which the central values of both are honoured and integrated.
    Stephen Batchelor, author of *After Buddhism*

Engaging in labour and radical politics is stressful and often involves conflict, and yet this seems necessary to bring about a world where all can flourish. Mike Slott is essential reading on how to ground effective socialist activism with a mindful approach to daily life.
    Mike Beggs, author of *The Blueprint* (Verso, forthcoming)

Marxism and Buddhism are two of the most powerful and enduring responses to human suffering, and have shaped many social movements and practices for transformation. This book offers a clearly-written and systematic attempt to develop a dialogue between the two in a western context. Activists and practitioners alike can benefit from engaging with the reflections offered.
    Laurence Cox, co-author of *The Irish Buddhist: The Forgotten Monk who Faced Down the British Empire*

Rooted in his own experience of political engagement and secular Buddhist practice, the author presents us with a carefully researched, lively and eloquent argument for uniting Marxist theory and activism with Buddhist insights and practices. A timely, persuasive and very useful contribution for the pursuit of social justice and personal fulfilment, I encourage everyone to read it.
    John Danvers, author of *Agents of Uncertainty; Interwoven Nature*

What has Buddhism got to do with socialism? In my experience, that's not a question widely asked on the U.S. left, so activists involved in labor or progressive politics should definitely check out Mike Slott's fascinating new study, *Mindful Solidarity*. The author is a longtime union activist and worker educator who makes the case for integrating the insights of Buddhist philosophy with secular radicalism.
    Steve Early, co-author of *Our Veterans: Winners, Losers, Friends and Enemies on the New Terrain of Veterans Affairs* and former International Representative, Communications Workers of America

Can toxic political and economic social structures be transformed solely by experiences of compassion and loving kindness arising from the meditation mat? Can efforts for progressive change really succeed when 'peace movements' are populated by activists struggling to digest their own anger, hatred and egotism? In *Mindful Solidarity*, Mike Slott answers both questions with a gentle but emphatic 'No' As an alternative, he offers a powerful, politico-spiritual synthesis informed by his personal experience of both activism and meditation – a rare combination.

>**David Edwards**, co-editor of the UK-based media watch site, Media Lens, and author of *A Short Book About Ego… And The Remedy of Meditation* (forthcoming)

Progressive politics works for social change. Buddhism focuses on individual change. Do they need each other? *Mindful Solidarity* brings them into a fruitful dialogue. Mike Slott's conclusion is persuasive: we need both.

>**David R. Loy**, author of *Ecodharma: Buddhist Teachings for the Ecological Crisis*

Mike Slott weaves together the core aspects of Secular Buddhism and Democratic Socialism, firmly establishing how their seemingly disparate themes are aligned. The result is a pragmatic roadmap for active change in the direction of a supportive, caring global society that moves from mere tolerance to mutual flourishing.

>**Ted Meissner**, Founder of the Secular Buddhist Association (USA)

A group of meditators and a group of activists walk into a book. Activists passionately express their visions and meditators share dharma understandings. *Mindful Solidarity* intertwines their voices, weaving discernment, cooperation, and guidance into every page.

>**Linda Modaro**, co-author of *Reflective Meditation: Cultivating Kindness and Curiosity in the Buddha's Company*

In *Mindful Solidarity* Mike Slott explores Buddhist wisdom and practice with a critical, creative and courageous eye from what he calls 'a secular, radical and socially engaged' perspective, in dialogue with Marxist thought and progressive social-political theories. He suggests we go beyond our personal quest for freedom from worldly suffering on the meditation cushion to cultivate an ethic of care and compassion that meets the complex challenges of the times we are living in.

    Carmel Shalev, author of In Praise of Ageing: Awakening to Old Age with Wisdom and Compassion

Mike Slott brings the conversation between Buddhism and radical politics into focus for twenty-first century activists as well as Buddhists looking to enhance their political engagement. *Mindful Solidarity* is clear, balanced, insightful, and deeply humane—required reading for anyone interested in the ways Buddhist ideas and practices might inspire our collective work towards building a better world—a world in which 'enlightenment' translates to 'flourishing for all'.

    James Mark Shields, author of *Against Harmony: Progressive and Radical Buddhism in Modern Japan*

Drawing on his own extensive involvement in political movements, the U.S. labor movement, and secular Buddhist theory and practice, Mike Slott makes a compelling case for a democratic socialist politics that is mindful and compassionate, that can bridge the gap between individual and social transformation, and that can envision a society which would make human flourishing possible for everyone.

    Karsten J. Struhl, author of *Interrogating Buddhist Philosophy* (forthcoming)

The exorbitant power of the few needs mindless division amongst the many. A mindful solidarity is its only antidote.

    Yanis Varoufakis, author of *Technofeudalism: What Killed Capitalism*

Integrating secular Buddhism with democratic socialism, Mike Slott provides practical insights for real-world challenges. *Mindful Solidarity* highlights the importance of ethical perspectives, offering valuable guidance for both activists and meditators.

    Jochen Weber, founder of Buddha-Stiftung, Germany

Mindful Solidarity
A Secular Buddhist Democratic Socialist Dialogue

Mike Slott

New York, Wellington and Sydney

First published in 2024 by Tuwhiri USA LLC
PO Box 3006, Montclair, NJ 07043, USA
and The Tuwhiri Project Ltd
13 Leith St, Gisborne 4010, Aotearoa New Zealand
www.tuwhiri.org & www.tuwhiri.nz

Mike Slott has waived royalty payments for this book
All proceeds will go to Tuwhiri USA LLC
This work is licensed under a Creative Commons Attribution-Non-Commercial-ShareAlike 4.0 International License

ISBN: 979-8-9909491-0-2 (US paperback)
ISBN: 979-8-9909491-4-0 (NZ paperback)
ISBN: 979-8-9909491-2-6 (ePub)

US Library of Congress Control Number: 2024912276

A catalogue record for this book is available from the
National Library of New Zealand
Kei te pātengi raraunga o Te Puna Mātauranga o Aotearoa
te whakarārangi o tēnei pukapuka

Book design by Ramsey Margolis & John Houston
Production by John Houston
Cover by minimum graphics
Cover images iStock

Set in IBM Plex Serif and Fira Sans
Printed in Aotearoa New Zealand by YourBooks and in other countries by IngramSpark

For Sharon, Sara, and Rosa L

Contents

Preface	xi
Introduction	xix

Part 1 - Foundations

1. Can You Be Both a Buddhist and a Marxist?	3
2. At the Crossroads of Individual and Social Transformation	23
3. The 'Truth' of Secular, Radically Engaged Buddhism	45

Part 2 - Critique

4. The Role and Goal of Meditation	65
5. Not-self and the Bodhisattava Path	89
6. Rethinking Left Politics	107

Part 3 - A Flourishing Life for All

7. Human Flourishing	129
8. The Five Core Tasks	151
9. In a Nutshell	169

A Note on Terminology	177
Acknowledgements	179
References	181
Notes	189
Name Index	195

Preface

October 1973. I was 20 years old, in my third year at a small liberal arts college near my home in Philadelphia, Pennsylvania. While I was a conscientious, engaged student in the subjects that I cared about – Philosophy, History, and Political Science – my energy and interest were increasingly bound up with radical, left-wing political activity. This was not a new direction for me but part of a gradual process of radicalization as I experienced in my teens the upheavals in American society and politics in the late 1960s and early 1970s: the civil rights and Black Power movements, the anti-Viet Nam war movement, and the failure of liberal Democrats to confront racism and a brutal war on the Vietnamese. Like many young people at the time, I had become thoroughly disillusioned with our system and looked for radical alternatives. So, I was quite happy when I was recruited to be a member of a chapter of the New American Movement (NAM), one of the many Left groups in the United States that emerged from the breakup of Students for a Democratic Society (SDS) in 1969. We were part of what would become known as the 'New Left', a broad assortment of radical organizations which believed that the 'Old Left', represented by the socialist and communist parties, needed to be supplanted by organizations which were committed to creating new forms of radical theory and praxis.

Our NAM chapter consisted of students like me, three professors from the college, and several people who lived in Philadelphia who had retained connections with the college. As a national organization, NAM was not a monolithic, centralized organization; local chapters had a variety of theoretical

Mindful Solidarity: A Secular Buddhist Democratic Socialist Dialogue

orientations and activities. Yet, there was a 'political glue' which held NAM together; namely, the belief in the need for a revolutionary transformation in the USA that was both thoroughly democratic and reflected the particular conditions in this country. The focus of our local group was twofold: education and debate about Marxist theories and engagement in the Philadelphia labor movement, primarily in the form of support for strikes and other labor protests. Our two major activities before the chapter broke up in 1975 involved support for a rank-and-file movement among Philadelphia taxi drivers and attempting to build a coalition to support striking bus drivers.

Aside from my studies, political involvement was thus the center of my life in 1973. It was how I defined myself and I envisaged a future of continuing and intensifying activism. If one of my friends or fellow political activists told me that they were reading a book that explored the ways in which core Buddhist insights and radical political perspectives were both essential and complemented each other, like the book you have in your hands, I would likely have responded with incredulity and disdain.

Buddhism? What does that have to do with the important work of making fundamental social change? The people I knew who were interested in Asian religions and alternative forms of spirituality were typically apolitical hippies who disdained materialism and commercialism, who sought to escape the problems of society rather than challenge repressive social institutions. At the worst, they were self-involved seekers of happiness and bliss who cared little about those who were poor and exploited. While my harsh assessment perhaps contained some element of truth, it was also because I had narrow blinders and the certainty of youth, leading to a sense of self-righteousness, and a relatively limited view of human beings and the nature of social change.

And yet, while my 20-year-old self was quite different from who I am now, I can also see how certain core assumptions and preferences that I held remain keystones in guiding the way I've lived my life and the perspectives that have most influenced me.

From a very young age, I developed a sense that all human beings

Preface

should have the opportunity to live a decent, flourishing life irrespective of their nationality, race, or income level. Growing up in a lower middle-class family that struggled financially at times, I was perhaps sensitized to notice how some people had more and better opportunities just because they had more money. This seemed fundamentally unfair. At the same time, when I was very young, we were one of the few Jewish families in our neighborhood. While we got along well with our Protestant and Catholic neighbors, I absorbed from my parents and relatives a kind of protectiveness and fear based on what had happened to Jews during the Holocaust and the continuing existence of anti-Semitism in the USA. The mistreatment of Jewish people led me to feel that the stereotypes of and discrimination against any nationality or race were unjustified. For that reason, the civil rights movement in the USA profoundly affected me as I identified with the struggle of African Americans for basic rights and a decent life. As I grew older, these core attitudes prompted me to look for a worldview or perspective that focused on the need for all human beings to be treated with respect and dignity, and to have an opportunity to have a decent, flourishing life.

After a brief period of interest in secular humanism in high school, I found in Marxism a perspective with such a universal approach. The kind of Marxism that I was attracted to, though, was non-dogmatic and open to criticism and change. I have always been wary of religions and political perspectives which claimed to have *The Truth*. My experience with Orthodox Jewish teachers who were preparing me for my Bar-Mitzvah when I was 13 years old exemplified this problem, and fostered a sense of the need for critical thinking and being able to express myself in my own voice. When I asked any questions which challenged religious doctrines, these teachers dismissed them and demanded that I accept the views and practices that they espoused. That just didn't sit right with me; I didn't like the idea of being told what to believe, what was right or wrong, simply out of adherence to a faith. That skepticism toward fixed doctrines and a distrust of religious leaders and teachers who demanded that I accept certain orthodoxies carried over to my encounter with Marxism.

I was not interested in a version of Marxism that put itself forward as having The Truth, requiring people to absorb a set of dogmatic beliefs and unconditionally follow a leader.

As I gravitated toward a humanistic, non-dogmatic Marxism which grounded itself in the day-to-day struggles of workers and offered a vision of a new kind of society, I found myself becoming impatient with theorizing that was divorced from real problems and struggles in society. Academic disputes which focused on terminology or minor conceptual differences among a small group of theorists, and which were disconnected from life's problems, seemed to me to be meaningless. The value of a political or philosophical perspective, I felt, resided in how it applied to our daily lives and how it enabled us to make life better for all human beings. In short, I developed the habit of judging perspectives based on their practical and ethical impact.

Finally, an enduring connection with my 20-year-old self is a gut-level belief that political perspectives and practices need to support and facilitate democracy in the fullest sense of the term. Looking back, I can see now that this orientation was initially a product of my personal, psychological history. Several times during my childhood, I had experienced the pain and trauma of events occurring which negatively impacted me and over which I had no 'voice' or say in the matter. Being left out of the loop in this way left a deep wound; and I believe this was the impetus, as I grew up, for my belief that everyone should have the right and opportunity to have a voice in determining their living and working conditions. People shouldn't be told what to do by others simply because they are in a position of authority. As I matured, this evolved into the notion that we need to create forms of collective and democratic deliberation in all areas and society.

These core, enduring sensibilities have guided my life's journey in the world of work and ideas. After college I continued my involvement in Left politics and became deeply engaged in the effort to make the US labor movement more democratic, militant, and progressive. I was a member of several unions for eight years and then eventually found work as a full-time union staff

Preface

person until my retirement at the end of 2017. Since 2001, I have also taught labor studies and labor history as an adjunct instructor at a university and been an active member and leader of our union. My 'home' continues to be in the labor movement. At the same time, I continue to explore and question Marxist theory not just in the context of debates among Marxists but in relation to other, non-Marxist perspectives. Among the most important of these have been Deweyan pragmatism and democratic theory, psychoanalysis, feminism, postmodernism, and anarchist notions of mutual cooperation. I have been drawn to dialogues between Marxism and each of these perspectives in which I try to understand similarities and differences between them, as well as the strengths and weaknesses of each. For me, this has been a fruitful way of developing an overall perspective which takes into account the complexity and diversity of human experience.

Buddhism was the last perspective and practice which became part of my ongoing exploration and dialogue, and it didn't occur because of some theoretical interest but because of a personal challenge. In 2010 I was going through a rough time due to work-related stress and found that my usual exercise routines and other forms of relaxation were not enough to reduce the pervasive anxiety that I experienced. At the urging of my wife, Sharon, who had some experience with Insight meditation, I began to practice mindfulness meditation, focused on the breath as the primary anchor. My initial foray into mindfulness meditation had a significant, positive impact and so I began a daily practice at the age of 57 which I've continued to this day. Having experienced how meditation reduced my anxiety, I began to explore the Buddhist perspectives and ideas underlying the practice. My wife and I connected with a local Insight meditation center and I felt a sense of kinship among practitioners who seemed committed to a dharma practice that was oriented toward mindfulness and compassion without the rituals and cultural trappings that are part of many of the traditional forms of Buddhism.

In this early stage of discovering Buddhism, a meditation teacher suggested that I read Stephen Batchelor's book, *Buddhism Without Beliefs*. I immediately felt a strong connection with Stephen's approach, as he not only moved away from reliance on rituals and orthodoxies but offered a fully secular and ethical interpretation of the insights and teachings of the historical Buddha, Gotama. At this point, I realized that secular Buddhism was a valuable perspective and practice which I wanted to integrate fully into my life. But how could I do this while maintaining my enduring commitment to a non-dogmatic, humanistic Marxism and several other perspectives? This was my key challenge.

And so, from 2011, I have focused on exploring the relationship between secular Buddhism and radical political perspectives, particularly a humanistic, non-dogmatic Marxism, in the form of a dialogical conversation between the two. I have analyzed their theories of human nature, society, and social change. I have looked at how each can offer supportive critiques of the other's perspectives and practices, pointing to limitations and gaps. I have examined how these perspectives can offer valuable insights and suggestions to each other, helping Buddhists to make the social dimension more integral to their practice, and supporting political activists in becoming more mindful and attuned to their 'inner' world so that they can be more effective activists. In general, I have tried to develop a secular, radically engaged approach to Buddhism which can contribute to a revived and more powerful radical political movement.

This book is the fruit of my ongoing dialogue, which will continue to evolve in the years ahead. Chapters 1 and 2 are based on two articles which appeared in the journal *Contemporary Buddhism*, though I significantly revised and updated the material. The other chapters in the book have their origins in blog posts and articles that I have written since 2011, initially for the Secular Buddhist Association, and then for the website of the Secular Buddhist Network (SBN). As editor of the SBN website, I and others involved in this project have tried to create a space for an open and respectful discussion of issues related to a secular approach to the dharma, as well as offering opportunities to create connections and a sense of community among practitioners. The website is not intended to be a platform for my particular interpretation of secular Buddhism. Instead, my colleagues and I understand the website and the affiliated online

Preface

groups to be just one of many efforts to develop a secular Buddhist trend which is relevant to our world today. We aim to foster a spirit of inclusiveness and dialogue as we co-create this new trend within Buddhism.

This non-dogmatic approach and an openness to other perspectives which we are fostering within the context of Buddhism is desperately needed in the broader movement for social and political change. If humanity is to address in a creative and humane way the key challenges of our time – the climate crisis, rampant social and economic inequality, violence and war, and various forms of discrimination and oppression – we must reject the notion that any one perspective or strategy has all the correct answers. A successful movement to create a society in which all can flourish will need to include a variety of liberatory perspectives rooted in both political and spiritual trends. Such an alliance will inevitably be marked by tensions and disputes over the means and ends of social transformation; this cannot be avoided. However, it is only by working through these disagreements in a comradely and compassionate way that we will be able to develop appropriate strategies and goals. In short, in line with the title of a book by the participatory educators Myles Horton and Paolo Freire, in developing secular Buddhism and other emancipatory perspectives, 'we are making the road by walking.'[1]

Introduction

I have a foot in two very different worlds: the global contemporary Buddhist community and the circle of Left labor and political activism. Very few of us have found a place in both worlds. While many western Buddhists are progressive in a general sense – liberals in the US parlance – they are generally not supportive of radical movements for social change and don't necessarily embrace a critique of neoliberal capitalism. Sometimes, that becomes painfully obvious. Jack Kornfield, one of the most well-known Insight meditation teachers in the US and a strong supporter of greater diversity within Buddhism, has developed close relationships with several corporate executives, including the executive chair of the Ford Motor Company, Bill Ford. During the 2023 strike by US autoworkers against the Ford Company and two other US automobile companies, Kornfield had a friendly discussion with Ford on the benefits of mindfulness for senior managers. In a discussion supposedly on the topic of 'right livelihood', as Katya de Kadt and I pointed out, Kornfield never raised with Ford the harm caused by his role in a profit-maximising company which exploits its workers and contributes to global warming and pollution.[2]

While there is some interest in Buddhism and meditation among younger activists, most people in Left labor and political movements are not engaged in the mindfulness and compassion practices of Buddhism. For some activists, Buddhism is, as it was for me for many years, a New-Agey trend that has no relevance to vitally needed political changes. At worst, it is seen as a distraction, taking activists away from their essential work and immersing them in a self-centered world of subjective experience. Other Left activists are just not aware of Buddhism and meditation; it is not on their radar screen.

In exploring a secular, radically engaged approach to Buddhism in this book, I am attempting to speak to participants in each world. To Buddhists, I say: I agree that we need to cultivate inner capacities of focus, mental integration, and insight through meditation; and we need to treat ourselves and others with compassion and love. I share these core values of mindfulness and compassion with you. Yet, the cultivation of meditative skills and an ethical stance cannot be fully developed in a society which harms people and reinforces greed and hatred. Further, while I respect followers of traditional Buddhism who believe in nirvana, karma, and rebirth, I believe that these notions distract us from any focus on trying to flourish in this life. To Left activists, I say: for my whole adult life I have been with you in the struggle for a democratic socialist society. I believe that capitalism and other systemic forms of oppression and exploitation need to be challenged by powerful mass movements, including a revived labor movement. I see the need for collective action. Yet, we cannot build a powerful mass movement for change if we don't recognize the ways in which our own tendencies toward greed and hatred, as well as a delusory belief in a separate, isolated self, not only cause harm to ourselves and others but create obstacles for Left movements to succeed. If we truly want to change society in meaningful ways, we need both individual and social transformation.

In the chapters that follow, I attempt to speak to both groups as I explore different aspects of a secular, radically engaged Buddhism. I begin by asking and answering the question: Can you be a Buddhist meditator and a democratic socialist who embraces a humanistic, non-dogmatic version on Marxism? I argue in Chapter 1 that a particular form of Buddhism and a certain type of Marxism do have important commonalities, but that there are also substantial differences between the two perspectives. Those differences can be fruitfully framed, however, as a conversation between two equally important ways of understanding human experience and social conditions. Brought together in this dialogical way, an understanding of Marxism can expand and deepen

Introduction

the spiritual-ethical practice of Buddhists, while a secular understanding of Buddhism can make radical political action more mindful, compassionate, and effective.

Chapter 2 continues this conversation but with an emphasis on revealing the limitations of ancestral Buddhist notions of human nature and social change. In this chapter I explicitly lay out the value of a secular, radically engaged approach to Buddhism which emerges in the dialogue between Buddhism and Marxism.

Chapter 3 focuses on a crucial aspect of a secular approach to the dharma: the move from truths to tasks as the cornerstone of a spiritual path. One of the most important aspects of Stephen Batchelor's secular Buddhism is his reformulation of the Four Noble Truths, the foundational statement of Buddhism, as four tasks or just one fourfold task. Based on his analysis of early Buddhist texts in the Pali Canon and the line of interpretation developed by the English-born Buddhist monk Ñāṇavīra Thera in the 1960s,[3] Batchelor argues that Gotama's insightful ethical and pragmatic teachings about how to live in this world were transformed into ontological truths as part of the emergence of the hierarchical religious institution that we in the west know as Buddhism. The Four Noble Truths constitute the essential truth claim of this religion. If we move from ontological truths to tasks, as Batchelor urges us to do, is there any meaningful role for a notion of truth in a secular approach? And if there is, how is this notion of truth different than the one found in conventional Buddhism? Finally, is the 'truth' of secular Buddhism more important or valuable than other important perspectives? I explore each of these questions in Chapter 3.

In Chapters 4 and 5, I contribute to the project of using a secular, radically engaged Buddhist perspective to 'rethink dharma', to examine critically and constructively key beliefs and practices of traditional Buddhism. In Chapter 4, I offer a critique of the role and goal of meditation as it's usually perceived and practiced by Buddhists in the west. For most western Buddhists, meditation provides the crucial context and practice to advance along the path. While meditation is vitally important, I argue that an overemphasis on meditation has led to an unfortunate de-emphasis of the ethical and socially-engaged dimension of Buddhism and facilitates an overly individualistic approach. Further, I critique the notion that the goal of meditation is to progress toward or attain some ultimate, nirvanic state or experience. For a secular, radically engaged Buddhist, the objective of meditation is to develop the skills and virtues which help us lead a more flourishing life and contribute to a society in which all people can flourish.

I continue this line of inquiry in Chapter 5, where I tackle other core beliefs in Buddhism: the notion that there are 'three marks of existence' that characterize reality; the view that one of those marks, not-self, means that we need to completely supplant our current sense of the self; and the idea that the bodhisattva is the model for how Buddhists should engage in the world.

In Chapter 6 I shine the analytical spotlight in the other direction, in an effort to 'rethink radical politics' and grapple with the problems and limits of Left political movements. Sadly, if one looks at the development of radical political parties and revolutionary movements from an historical perspective, one discerns a pervasive tendency for idealism and solidarity to be increasingly replaced by authoritarianism and unethical behavior. This has led to constant schisms and internal conflicts within the Left that have damaged its potential to transform society. At the same time, movements purporting to fight for human liberation can themselves become agents of repression and harm. I explore how a secular, radically engaged Buddhist approach can play a vital role in helping Left political movements function more effectively and stay aligned with their core values. For individuals involved in Left politics, secular Buddhist practice can foster a form of political agency which is mindful, compassionate, and sustains activism for the long road ahead, with all its ups and downs. Finally, I discuss the specific roles that Left activists informed by secular Buddhism can play in the broader Left movements.

The notion of human flourishing appears constantly in Chapters 1 through 6. Human flourishing, the creation of an ethical, meaningful life, is an essential element of a secular, radically engaged Buddhist approach. But what does human flourishing mean and what are the forms of human flourishing?

Introduction

What are the internal or individual conditions for flourishing, and what are the external or social ones? In Chapter 7, I offer a perspective on human flourishing or *eudaimonia* based on Aristotle's theory of human *telos*, Gotama's core teachings, Marx's notion of human nature and praxis, and Martha Nussbaum's capabilities approach. By integrating the ideas of Aristotle, Gotama, Marx, and Nussbaum on human flourishing, we can begin to grasp the diversity of human experience and human potentials while recognizing the internal and social conditions needed to foster flourishing.

Having explored the ways in which a secular, radically engaged Buddhist approach can make radical political action more mindful, compassionate, and efficacious, as well as the role of secular Buddhists within political groups, I consider in Chapter 8 the broader question: What are the key tasks in life for secular, radically engaged Buddhists? Here, I extend and revise Stephen Batchelor's reinterpretation of the Four Noble Truths to four tasks to propose five essential tasks for someone who seeks not just individual transformation and flourishing, but the creation of a society in which the opportunity and supports for flourishing are offered to all human beings, in ways which recognize our interdependence and vital connection with other beings, and the ecosystem as a whole. These five tasks were originally developed in an article I co-wrote with my dharma buddies and activist comrades, Katya de Kadt and Karsten Struhl.[4] In that article, we offered the five tasks in an outline form; in this chapter, I develop and expand our perspective.

Finally, in Chapter 9, I provide a concise summary of a secular, radically engaged approach in the form of twelve propositions. I offer them not as universal, timeless statements but as a snapshot of where my explorations of Buddhism and radical politics have led to at this point. I hope they provoke the reader to identify and assess your own perspectives on the human experience, the values you hold most dear, and the kind of life you wish to see for yourself and others. May you do this, as I hope I have done, with compassion, humility, and a clear-minded sense of both our human limitations and our great potential for creating a flourishing life for all.

Part 1
Foundations

Chapter 1

Can You Be Both a Buddhist and a Marxist?

On the surface, this seems a rather odd question.[5] Buddhism is an Asian religion that is over twenty-five hundred years old, one which became one of the most important spiritual traditions in the world. Marxism is a radical theoretical perspective, the basis for political movements which emerged in the mid-nineteenth century, in the context of the development of industrial capitalism and the struggle between working people and the capitalist class in western Europe. Buddhism is a spiritual path that aims to end suffering and attain nirvana; Marxism addresses the collective effort to change the economic and political conditions in which we all live. Different aims, a focus on different aspects of life. How can they possibly be connected? Yet, this is precisely the question that absorbed me after I encountered meditation and Buddhism at a relatively late age, after many years as a labor and political activist.

I am not the first to explore the relationship between these two seemingly divergent perspectives. Several writers have insightfully identified some common elements in Buddhism and Marxism, as well as important differences, including Brien, Struhl, and Priest.[6]

With respect to commonalities, both perspectives emphasize the need to critique superficial, common sense ways of understanding reality, and to grasp the underlying processes and structures which shape our lives. They are both radical in the sense of going to the root of causes and prescribing a fundamental transformation in the ways in which we understand and act in the world. Second, both stress the need to understand the primacy of change and process in human experience in order to respond wisely. Third, and perhaps most important, Buddhism and Marxism share similar humane goals: the alleviation of suffering and the development of the so-called true or better aspects of our human nature. In this context, they each provide a diagnosis and a remedy for what ails us. Finally, their diagnosis and remedies are meant to apply to all human beings; they are perspectives which offer a universal path to human flourishing.

At the same time, Buddhism and Marxism differ in important respects in addition to those noted above. Buddhism focuses on the examination of internal experiences (sensations, feelings, emotions, and thoughts) while economic and political structures and processes are central to Marxist theories. Buddhism is about the existential-psychological dimension of life while Marxism is about the social and collective dimension, primarily in the realm of work and economic production. And finally, the context and primary source for radical change in Buddhism is the individual; the basis for change in Marxism is the struggle between social classes.

It would be tempting to try to develop some new synthesis – Buddhist Marxism or Marxist Buddhism – but that is not my aim. Rather, I think a more fruitful approach is to bring these perspectives together in a dialogue which enables us to discern the elements in each which can help us experience better lives and be more effective political activists. This is similar to the approach taken by Laurence Cox. He believes that Buddhism and Marxism provide respectively a 'grammar of spiritual practice' and a 'grammar of social movements' that enable us to understand better personal development and political struggles. Their limitations and value are highlighted by confronting each perspective with the other; through such a dialogue, it then becomes evident that what Buddhist practitioners and Left activists are each working for cannot be attained unless each group recognizes the insights of the other perspective.[7]

In holding each perspective up to the light of the other and mutually interrogating each other, we find that both Buddhism and Marxism have strengths and weaknesses in helping us to understand human experience and social problems. Buddhism provides us with profound insights about the human condition. Based on these understandings, Buddhism identifies those practices which lead to greater happiness and less suffering in response to existential challenges that we all must face as mortal human beings, irrespective of the particular family, society, or historical era that we live in. But while Buddhism captures certain basic aspects of universal human experience, it does not take account of the interaction or dialectic between humans qua social beings and the social structures and processes that humans both reinforce and challenge in the course of history. That dialectic is the province of a radical social theory which grasps the root causes of social harms and suffering: Marxism. At the same time, however, Marxism does not address the ways in which, at an experiential level, life causes suffering and anguish irrespective of the social context.

Defining Buddhism and Marxism

To explore this issue in more detail, I first need to define what I mean by Buddhism and Marxism. When I use the term 'Buddhism' in this book, I am referring to what Ken Jones has characterized as the 'core dharma' or essential aspects of conventional Buddhism, which includes the 'basic diagnosis of the human condition, the prescription of meditative practices and the goal of existential awakening (i.e., enlightenment).' That core is composed of the following foundational elements:[8]

- ☆ The Four Noble Truths:
  1) There is suffering in the world; 2) Craving, rooted in the delusion of a separate self, is the cause of suffering; 3) We can cease suffering and attain a state of nirvana if we abandon craving; and 4) There is an eightfold path, based on a set of virtues, skills, and understandings to be realized, which enables us to attain nirvana.
- ☆ The three marks or essential aspects of existence: impermanence; suffering; and not-self.

- ☆ The three fires or afflictive states which trap us in suffering: greed and hatred (the dual aspects of craving), and delusion (based on the illusion of a separate self).
- ☆ Dependent co-origination: the notion that everything that exists is conditioned, dependent on something else. Nothing exists independently.
- ☆ The five moral precepts:
  1) to abstain from taking life; 2) to abstain from taking what is not given; 3) to abstain from sensuous misconduct; 4) to abstain from false speech; and 5) abstain from intoxicants (alcohol, drugs, etc.) as tending to cloud the mind.
- ☆ Karma as a psychological and naturalistic phenomenon: Actions are naturally followed by consequences, not as the result of divine judgement. Actions lead inevitably to appropriate consequences.

When I refer to Buddhism or Buddhists, I am referring to these core elements. When I discuss a particular trend or view within Buddhism, I will note that this trend or view is not shared by all Buddhists.

Marxism, too, is a complex and diverse body of thought and practice. I will similarly be using the term 'Marxism' based on a set of core propositions shared by all Marxists. First, Marxists believe that the production and reproduction of our material existence is both the basis for and the key (although not the only) factor in structuring society. In the context of this notion – often referred to as historical materialism – Marxists further argue that historical development is significantly shaped by the conflict between social groups or classes over the ownership and control of the means of production and reproduction. Third, because of class conflict and other internal contradictions within a particular mode of production, Marxists assert that socio-economic formations inevitably become unstable and incapable of being fixed or reformed.

Fourth, capitalism, the dominant socio-economic formation of the last several hundred years, is prone to crises due to tendencies inherent in the nature of profit-driven competition between businesses, as well as conflict between the two most significant social groups: working class people and the owners of businesses, the capitalist class. Fifth, given their common experiences of mistreatment and exploitation, groups of workers (particularly in individual companies) tend to band together into collective organizations such as unions to defend and advance their interests vis-à-vis their employer. When workers move beyond sectional economic solidarity and gain a broader political understanding of their role in society, they have the potential to be the primary agent of a fundamental transformation of capitalism, one in which workers and their allies supplant the capitalist class and create a democratic, non-exploitative society.

Finally, Marxists believe that progress in history, whether it be in the realm of technology, culture, economics, or politics, is based on our inherent and distinctive capacity for creative, purposive labor. Marx called this praxis. Ultimately, change is only possible because of this unique human capacity.

Given the wide range of Marxist theories and Marxist-inspired political movements, these core propositions have been interpreted and applied in various ways. Nonetheless, it is important to initially define a core set of Marxist propositions, as I have done for Buddhism, to bring these two perspectives into a conversation with each other.

Now, there are several ways in which such a dialogue can be enacted. Karsten Struhl insightfully uses the Four Noble Truths as the vehicle to examine how each perspective explains human suffering and how it can be remedied.[9] I am following a different approach here. I discuss how each perspective envisages an ideal society in which human beings can flourish, live in harmony, and actualize our best human potentials – or in the famous phrase of US President Abraham Lincoln, which later became the title of a book by Steven Pinker, 'the better angels of our nature'.[10] I then show for each how the other perspective reveals limitations in that ideal vision based on an important aspect of human experience.

Marxist ideal, Buddhist reality

Marx himself was famously critical of attempts by theorists and political parties to lay out a plan for a socialist society based on a set of abstract ideas; he derisively called this trend 'Utopian Socialism'.[11] The form of any emerging socialist society would depend on the specific historical circumstances attending this transition in each case. But while Marx thus avoided presenting a detailed vision of what a socialist society would be like, the overall parameters and key elements of such a society can be discerned from comments that he and socialists who followed him have made. It is in this sense that we can speak of a desirable society for Marxists and explore the limits to creating such a society that Buddhist insights reveal.

This society has been referred to in various ways, reflecting the various trends within the Marxist tradition: communism with a small c, democratic socialism, workers' democracy, etc. Whatever the appellation, such a society has certain basic characteristics. In the first place, it is a society in which human beings have the opportunity to develop their full human potential for intelligent, purposive, and creative activity. Further, natural, socio-economic, and cultural resources are used for the benefit of all the people, not the profit of a few.

In this society, every human being is guaranteed the material necessities of life, an adequate income, health security, and the opportunity to gain education and training. In this way, everyone enjoys equal life chances. Exploitative and oppressive social relationships are eliminated, allowing human beings to interact with each other on the basis of mutual respect and justice. In this egalitarian society, it is the content of one's character that is essential, not one's skin color or who one's family is.

To the extent that such a complex society requires policies to be chosen, planning to occur, and the administration and regulation of human activities, it is not a bureaucracy or an elite group that is in charge. Instead, working people, through their participation in and control of various democratic social institu-

Chapter 1 Can You Be Both a Buddhist and a Marxist?

tions (unions, community planning boards, representative assemblies) make the key decisions in society. In short, this society is a substantive democracy whose resources are owned, controlled, and utilized by and for all the people.

Put aside for the moment the question of whether such a society, or even some relatively close approximation, can actually be established sometime in the future. Try to imagine the life of an individual in such a society. Because a democratic socialist society would be organized to support human flourishing, many of the problems that make our current life so difficult would no longer play a significant role. Insecurity would be reduced as people are guaranteed the basic necessities of life. Competition and striving for advantage over others would also be less prominent in a world in which everyone experiences nurture and support for their human potential. The horrors of war, famine, and environmental devastation would disappear, allowing us to lead lives marked by peace, comfort, and security. Technology and automation would be used to free human beings from uncreative, dangerous and physically difficult labor while reducing the total amount of time needed to work. We would have more time to spend with our families and friends, as well as to develop our talents and interests in a variety of areas. Marx envisaged the full development of human potential in this context in these terms:

> ... in communist society, where nobody has one exclusive sphere of activity but each can become accomplished in any branch he wishes, society regulates the general production and thus makes it possible for me to do one thing today and another tomorrow, to hunt in the morning, fish in the afternoon, rear cattle in the evening, criticise after dinner, just as I have a mind, without ever becoming hunter, fisherman, herdsman or critic.[12]

A wonderful world and surely anyone would wish to be part of it. So, would we be happy and content? Certainly, happier than now – and that is, of course, no minor accomplishment. However, there would still be aspects of life that would cause us anguish and suffering, in spite of these optimal conditions for social interaction and the development of our potential. This is the point at which Marxism reaches its limit.

Let's start with the most obvious and important existential fact. We are mortal beings. We are going to die and virtually all of us – unless condemned to death at a particular date and time – do not know when we will die. This is an inescapable fact of life, an existential certainty regardless of the society we live in. For most of us, the inevitability of our death is a source of suffering and anguish. We do not want to die; we are, as living beings, 'hard-wired' to want to survive. And yet, we are painfully conscious of our own mortality. The thought of our death is frightening. Worse, we know that dying is not, for most people, some pleasant slide to oblivion. Many of us will experience physical and mental pain before we die. For the lucky few, the process of dying may be relatively quick, following a long period of creative activity, loving relationships, and meaningful social contributions. Unfortunately, the vast majority of human beings face a fairly protracted period in which our body (and perhaps our mind as well) loses its ability to function in ways that are both painful and sometimes degrading.

But it is not just our mortality, our impermanence, that is troubling to us. Even when we are relatively physically and mentally fit, we suffer daily. As human beings, we have needs and desires that are not met. We experience fears and aversions for objects, people, and events. We are often restless and bored. In short, in a multitude of ways throughout our existence, life is not what we wish it to be. Life inevitably brings us suffering; à la Elizabeth Barrett Browning's famous sonnet on love,[13] let me count some of the most common ways that Gotama recognized that we suffer:

☆ The things and people we want, we don't get.
☆ The things and people we don't want, we get.
☆ The things and people we have and we wanted suddenly change and we no longer want them.

Chapter 1 Can You Be Both a Buddhist and a Marxist?

☆ We lose the things and people that we have and we wanted.
☆ We learn that what we wanted and we got is not good for us.
☆ We learn that what we don't have is good for us.
☆ We inevitably experience sickness, injuries, and aging as a part of life.

What Buddhism recognizes is that we suffer because we are human beings who have needs, wants, aversions, and fears in a world in which it can never be possible for us to have all that is 'good for us' all the time. More precisely, we suffer because we get attached to and hooked on needs, wants, fears, and aversions which are only the projections of our illusions and conditioning. In Buddhist terms, we crave pleasant or good experiences, not recognizing their impermanence and our relative lack of control over what happens in our life. Craving and the delusion of a separate self or 'me' cause us to experience suffering beyond the inevitable pains of life.

Now, of course, we also have many moments of happiness in our life as well. Buddhists understand the experience of happiness, but they also know that happiness is impermanent, as is everything else. It is that impermanence of events, objects, and people that is difficult for us to understand and embrace. As beings who must survive in the world, we have a naturally strong tendency to hold on to what makes us feel good and to recoil from what we experience as bad. Yet it is precisely this tendency to attach ourselves to what pleases us, and retreat from unpleasant objects, events, and people, that causes us to suffer. What is, in one respect, an essential survival mechanism for a biological being living in an uncertain, perilous world, is also that which makes human life difficult, in any kind of society, and sometimes almost unbearable.

So, from the Buddhist perspective, the Marxist notion of an ideal society fails to take into account certain facts of human experience and human tendencies which constitute obstacles to a democratic socialist society in which all human beings can flourish. We cause harm to ourselves and each other not just because social institutions are oppressive and exploitative, but because of our deeply rooted patterns of thought, emotions, and behavior. Unless we transform ourselves to uproot these patterns, we will continue to suffer as individuals and in the context of social institutions.

Buddhist ideal, Marxist reality

Thus, for Buddhists, to create an ideal society in which compassion, care, and peace characterize social interactions, individuals need to change their understanding of the human condition and their way of being in the world. Our own suffering and the suffering we cause to others can only end when we no longer attach to or recoil from unpleasant objects, events, and people, and when we understand the illusion of a separate self. To be free of attachment and aversion, one must understand impermanence, insubstantiality, and interconnectedness and engage in certain practices, including meditation and ethical acts rooted in care and concern, which facilitate our path to a state of non-attachment and non-aversion. Of course, the ultimate goal for traditional Buddhists is to achieve a state of enlightenment or nirvana based on being free of attachments and aversions. Many contemporary Buddhists in the west, however, put to the side this metaphysical belief in transcendence and instead emphasize that committing oneself to practice meditation and to act ethically leads to less suffering, and creates the basis for a society in which people treat each other with respect and care.

In this sense, Buddhist practice is not just about attaining peace and calm, a purity of mind, in order to edify the individual soul. When we understand why we suffer and know how to lessen suffering, we naturally want to lessen the suffering of others. In our dealings with others, we thus act with loving friendliness (*metta*, in Pali) and compassion. Contrary to the view asserted by Žižek, that western Buddhism essentially functions as a means to allow individuals to tolerate the insanity and brutality of globalized capitalism,[14] there is an inherently social and ethical dimension to Buddhism.

While Buddhism thus has an inherently social dimension, Buddhists believe that the root cause of human suffering, as well as the remedy, reside in the individual's experience with and response to their perceived experience. We

Chapter 1 Can You Be Both a Buddhist and a Marxist?

need to work on changing ourselves, understanding the causes of suffering and following the eightfold path, which includes meditative practices, ethical actions, and wisdom. A human being who cultivates these understandings, skills, and virtues will act more skillfully toward others. As more and more people act in this way, social relationships will become more peaceful, just, and empathetic. A society in which loving kindness is the primary basis of social relationships is one in which the vast majority understand and act based on non-attachment and compassion. This is the path to the ideal society according to Buddhism.

There is an important kernel of truth in the notion (not limited to Buddhism of course) that social change requires a fundamental change in individual behavior, attitudes, and understandings. On the most basic level, when we show kindness and generosity to others, they tend to react positively and, in turn, will likely show more kindness and generosity to others. Acts of loving friendliness and compassion are 'infectious' in this sense.

Two small examples from my own life: I remember one time when I went to a cafe to get a coffee after having had a very pleasant and rewarding time with someone. I went to the cashier to pay for my coffee and she said, 'You have such a nice smile on your face.' I wasn't aware of my facial expression, but I could see that my good mood had lifted her spirits as well. Another time I was trying to get into a parking lot and an endless stream of traffic going the other way caused me to wait longer than I wanted. Feeling increasingly impatient, I began to focus on what I needed to do and how I hated to drive on that street. But then, a driver coming in the opposite direction slowed down and motioned for me to make the left turn into the parking lot. He smiled at me and I felt a palpable relief and a sense of calm returning. As I walked the steps up to my office, I felt lighter and more capable of responding positively to others.

And yes, beyond these small but precious moments in life, individual actions imbued with mindful, loving friendliness can have an even broader social impact. In recent years, a trend has developed within Buddhism that emphasizes the social action implications of Gotama's teachings. Advocates of 'engaged Buddhism', such as the contributors to the books edited by Kotler,

McLeod, and Queen, assert that compassion and care for others need to manifest in all areas of life: from personal interactions to providing service to those in need, to involvement in activist groups fighting for peace, an ecologically sustainable economy, and social justice. Guided by an ethic of non-harming and compassion, such Buddhists strive to reduce suffering caused by both the existential conditions of life and social conditions that harm people.[15]

While individual actions underpin social transformation, we must also recognize, as Marxists do, the complex, dialectical relationship between individual actions and social institutions. In the first place, each individual is shaped, partially constituted, by obdurate social structures. Even Buddhists who assert the need for collective action and radical political change, such as Ken Jones, fail to appreciate this dimension of the individual-society relationship. Thus, Jones argues that:

> it is our root existential condition that is primary. It is from this that our social condition originates, and the radical remedy for the ills of that social condition depends on no less a radical change in the kind of people we typically are.[16]

The quality and character of society doesn't primarily arise from the thoughts and actions of individuals. There exists in this world a whole complex of powerful economic, political, and social structures. These structures stubbornly persist because they sustain and promote the interests of specific groups of people, namely economic and political elites. Further, the vast majority of us internalize the structures and cultural norms of our existing society, thus creating habits of obedience and passivity within hierarchies which reinforce their hegemonic power. As a result, these structures have a 'hardness', a relative permanence, that makes them extremely resistant to change. If it is true that the world is, as Buddhists emphasize, marked by constant change and impermanence, it is also the case that some aspects of our social reality are relatively immovable and unchanging.

Chapter 1 Can You Be Both a Buddhist and a Marxist?

At the same time, in the interaction or dialectic between the individual and society, there are certain capacities of human beings that are also relatively enduring irrespective of the social context. This is the sense in which Marx understood the human condition. As Norman Geras in his book, *Marx and Human Nature,* has pointed out, Marx views creative, intelligent activity (praxis) as one of the distinctive capacities of human beings, and thus a core element of human nature.[17] Yet, just as Gotama rejected the notion of a substantial self or soul, Marx does not conceive of praxis as a transcendent, permanent, and fixed property of an essential self. In the first place, while praxis is part of the set of human capacities which are the product of our biological evolution, praxis can only be actualized in a social context; consequently, it is a mistake to conceive of praxis abstracted from social interaction. Moreover, since we are the product both of biological evolution and socio-cultural development, the fact that praxis is part of our human nature does not mean that we should view it as transcendent and immutable.

Thus, we can reject the idea of a universal human essence, separate from social interaction, and still recognize that there are enduring capacities that play a fundamental role in shaping the processes and structures of society. In addition to our capacity for praxis, we naturally seek what we want and need and are averse to what we don't want and need. Beyond that, we partake in a universal human tendency for aggression, competition, and dominance, just as we enjoy a human capacity for rationality, generosity, care, and empathy. We have a tendency to view the 'Other' as less than us and/or a threat, just as we can perceive another person or group from their own vantage point, in a compassionate way.

These relatively enduring human capacities interact with relatively hard social structures. We grow up in a society that emphasizes competition, domination, and avarice; and so those aspects of our nature develop within and through such a social context. In turn, individual behaviors reinforce and reproduce the very same oppressive social structures based on these qualities. And yet, as Marxists have emphasized, we have, through forms of praxis which facilitate human flourishing and other positive, life-affirming capacities, the potential to change and transform oppressive social structures. If we didn't, how can one explain progress (admittedly in its varied and contradictory forms), social revolutions, the increasing legitimacy of democracy, etc.?

This complex dialectic is a core element of Marxist social theory. As Marx said:

> The premises from which we begin are not arbitrary ones. ... They are the real individuals, their activity and the material conditions under which they live, both those which they find already existing and those produced by their activity.[18]

A radical social theory like Marxism helps us understand the hardness of social structures and the broad spectrum of human capacities that cause us to both reproduce and transform those structures. In contrast, Buddhism envisages social change primarily as a one-way causal interaction: changes in the individual's mind and behavior lead to social changes. It's true that we need to change ourselves as part of the process of social change, but that is only part of the solution. Social structures are not transformed solely by individual acts of compassion and loving kindness.

What is also required are collective forms of struggle and collective organizations that challenge social structures which are highly resistant to change. This is so for two reasons. First, institutional forms of power and dominance can only be challenged and ultimately transformed by alternative institutional forms. Capitalists' exploitation can only be countered by the collective action of workers, through unions and political organizations. A tyranny can only be overthrown by a mass organization of citizens. Further, while changes in our selves do have an impact on our social relationships and the larger society, the reverse is also true; changes in individuals can be the product of collective activity. Marx emphasized this point: only by engaging in collective struggles against exploitation and oppression can working people develop the individual skills and broader perspectives which enable them to transform the system and create a worker-run economy and a democratically-controlled society.

In sum, the Buddhist prescription for personal happiness and an ideal society lacks one key ingredient: an understanding of the relatively durable social conditions that block our ability to limit suffering and live happy, fulfilled lives. At the same time, the Marxist vision of an ideal society elides the stubborn, existential facts of human suffering, as well as failing to recognize those aspects of ourselves which create obstacles to a socialist transition. Yet, both perspectives also provide us with valuable insights about how all human beings can attain a good life.

How Buddhism enriches radical political activity

For a radical political activist, the value of Buddhism is, in the first place, that it sets a realistic boundary on the exclusively social dimension of Marxism. To whatever extent a decent, just society can be created, people will still suffer. We cannot create a perfect society and we should not claim that we can. Consequently, the hubris that sometimes pervades radical social theory (' "X theory" will solve all of our problems.') will be mitigated, and partially replaced with a greater sense of humility and a clearer understanding of the obstacles to social transformation.

Second, the cultivation of non-attachment and loving friendliness, core components of the Buddhist tradition, can help activists be more effective and sustain a long-term commitment to social change. Some people argue that recognizing the impermanence of things and events, as well as feeling a powerful compassion for others, would weaken or dilute an activist's passion and lead to a devaluation of political activism. In fact, the opposite is true. When activism is less fueled by rage and aggression which are aimed at harming the enemy or the 'Other', we can better confront exploitative social structures and those in power. Our ability to develop workable strategies will be increased insofar as we 'keep our eyes on the prize' rather than have our vision clouded by aversion and anger linked to the needs of our egos. In addition, a Buddhist perspective helps us to go through the hard times and difficult defeats that we must inevitably encounter. The Buddhist emphasis on impermanence and the conditioned nature of all human acts provides us with a more long-term perspective on the day-to-day struggles. We can lose a battle that we care deeply about, and feel badly, but that does not shake our core commitment.

Finally, if one looks at the development of radical political parties and revolutionary movements from an historical perspective, there is a pervasive tendency for idealism and solidarity to be replaced over time by authoritarianism and unethical behavior. Certainly, establishing and maintaining democratic structures that ensure the accountability of leaders and due process can constrain corrupting tendencies. Just as important, however, a Buddhist-inspired sense of loving friendliness and non-attachment would provide additional support for honest and egalitarian modes of interaction. If our actions within an organization are less determined by ego-based desire, anger, and delusion, we are more likely to make a productive contribution and treat others with greater respect and dignity.

How Marxism enriches Buddhist practice

At the same time, a Marxist perspective can have a salutary impact on Buddhist practice. Consider meditation, which for many western Buddhists is the heart of their practice. It is common for Buddhists to identify the 'monkey mind' – the frantic succession of thoughts and emotions dominated by aversions, desires, and delusions which often appears as an unwelcome visitor during our meditation periods – as a key impediment to cultivating meditative skills. This is certainly true. Yet, Buddhists often fail to see that meditation can be seriously impeded by other obstacles besides the monkey mind or other 'internal' hindrances. Like all other human activities, meditation takes place within a social context and presupposes certain material conditions. To start with the most obvious example, most of us can only meditate when we have had enough nutrition to sustain the mental and physical effort required. We also need to have time to set aside for meditation. We need a relatively comfortable and

Chapter 1 Can You Be Both a Buddhist and a Marxist?

quiet space as well. As Virginia Woolf noted in the context of the challenges faced by women writers, one needs a room of one's own. Finally, it is extremely difficult to meditate if we are experiencing any form of social, psychological, or physical coercion. In extreme situations, the notion of meditation seems almost unreal. How does one meditate while facing imminent threats to one's life? In short, if we believe that meditation is a crucial element of a happier and more fulfilled life, we must pay close attention to the social and material circumstances under which human beings engage in that process.

There is another way that Marxism can enrich Buddhist practice. In evaluating human behavior, Buddhists often contrast skillful versus unskillful actions. When our actions are skillful, grounded in mindfulness, wisdom, and compassion, they lead to happiness and a lessening of suffering; unskillful actions based on desire, aversion, and delusion have the opposite effects. For Buddhists, skillful actions primarily pertain to the individual's relationship to himself/herself and to others. We are skillful when we learn how to observe mindfully our own aversions, desires, and delusions. We act skillfully when we respond with friendliness to a person who has harmed us in some way. If, as I've suggested, many obstacles to a lessening of suffering and a happier life arise from the negative impact of exploitative and oppressive social structures, then the scope of skillful actions must be broadened to include ways in which the negative effect of such structures is mitigated, and ultimately transformed. We ought, then, to view skillful actions as including a broader continuum of activity, ranging from ways we work on ourselves, to interpersonal actions, to community organizing struggles, to strategies to displace and subvert the hegemony of the capitalist class – a key focus of the Italian Marxist, Antonio Gramsci.[19]

Paying greater attention to the importance of skillful actions at the macro level requires us to examine more closely how we function in the world of work (paid or unpaid). As part of the eightfold path (the fourth of the Four Noble Truths), 'right livelihood' means that we should earn a living in an ethical way, and that wealth should be gained legally and peacefully. Thus, arms trading, prostitution, and drug dealing are specifically ruled out, as are other occupations that cause one to violate the principles of right speech and action. In practice, this has meant that any job that doesn't directly cause harm is acceptable. However, if we understand that the social and structural constraints to happiness are as crucial as individual and interpersonal ones, then we need to add to the list of harmful occupations. From this perspective, harm includes not just direct damage, but contributing to the perpetuation of harmful social structures. An example: Is a financial speculator on Wall Street engaged in a right livelihood? I think not; whatever their progress in gaining mindfulness in meditation or their good works toward others, financial speculation epitomizes the way in which our economy puts profits before human needs, leading to the privation, alienation, and exploitation of the vast majority of people.

Of course, the difficulty lies not in identifying the most egregious cases of occupations that cause social harming. Between a social worker and a nuclear bomb manufacturer lies a whole range of jobs for which the criteria of individual and social harming are not so easily applied. All of us, no matter what social role we play, are, in some sense, complicit in the continued functioning of our socio-economic system. The issue is not one of establishing a rigid Buddhist-Marxist test for occupational correctness, but of recognizing that right livelihood has a social dimension that goes beyond direct harming. This recognition needs to be incorporated into a Buddhist perspective as well.

A fruitful dialogue

I have offered some ideas for how Buddhism and Marxism can enrich each other and consequently make their respective practices more fruitful. Our actions need to be guided by the mutual interaction of loving kindness and mindfulness on the one hand, and on the other, solidarity and a critical social analysis. We need both approaches if we want to reduce suffering and facilitate the flourishing of all human beings.

Those of us who find that Buddhism and Marxism resonate with our personal history, as well as our intellectual and political interests, confront

Chapter 1 Can You Be Both a Buddhist and a Marxist?

the question, Can you be both a Buddhist and a Marxist? Yes, but it depends on what kind of Marxist and what kind of Buddhist you are. On the one hand, a Marxist for whom all human problems are the product of socio-economic structures and processes will see Buddhism as just another religion that offers people consolation in a world of suffering. On the other, a Buddhist who disengages from social action, focusing primarily on meditative practices as the solution to suffering, will view Marxism as an unskillful perspective based on anger, delusion and egoism. If we reject these forms of Marxism and Buddhism, we can live with integrity and without contradiction, as someone for whom Buddhist insights and practice, and Marxist theory and activism, converge as complementary aspects of one's life. When we understand how Buddhist and Marxist perspectives can enrich each other, we gain crucial conceptual tools and valuable practices which enable us to become happier and more fulfilled at an individual level, while becoming more effective and mindful in the realm of progressive political action.

While Buddhism and Marxism can fruitfully complement each other, there are other world views and practices that address the existential and political dilemmas we experience as human beings. Each person has to find his or her own path. The Dalai Lama expressed this well when he said:

> Of course, to myself, Buddhism is the best. But this does not mean that Buddhism is best for the world. No! Each person, each individual can find the best. Like medicine, you cannot say 'Just because I take it, it is the best medicine'. For some people, Christian is best because it is most effective.[20]

Within many religious, spiritual, and political traditions, there are philosophical perspectives, beliefs, and practices that promote both human compassion and the kind of society advocated by Marx in which the 'free development of each is the condition for the free development of all'.[21] For Christians, the Catholic social teaching of the 'preferential option for the poor', as well as the prophetic, liberatory dimension of certain Protestant denominations, have supported a radical political stance. The Jewish notion of *tikkun* (repairing the world) offers similar resources. Likewise, political movements based on anarchist, feminist, and ecological perspectives can foster loving kindness and solidarity. Thus, someone who seeks to experience a fulfilled, reasonably happy life, and wants to contribute to radical political change, can find other perspectives that provide inspiration and guidance. In the context of a complicated, diverse world, this tolerant, pragmatic yet visionary sensibility offers us the soundest basis for living together and transforming society.

Chapter 2

At the Crossroads of Individual and Social Transformation

Buddhism and Marxism can enrich each other's perspectives and practices if we bring them into a dialogue with each other.[22] But what kind of Buddhism emerges from this interchange? One approach to answering this question would be to integrate a radical Marxist perspective with an existing tradition within Buddhism. In his article, 'Zen Marxism', Paul Shackley attempts to do just that, highlighting common areas of agreement between Zen and Marxism.[23] This is not the approach that I have taken; as a lifelong secular agnostic, I was never drawn to any of the ancestral lineages of Buddhism. Instead, I have explored this question by bringing together two increasingly prominent trends in western Buddhism: secular Buddhism and an 'engaged' Buddhism oriented toward radical social change. Secular Buddhism, as articulated by Stephen Batchelor[24] and others, has sought to jettison the cultural accretions and transcendent, divine entities that developed as part of the various Asian Buddhisms, while embracing Gotama's analysis of and remedy for human suffering. Socially engaged Buddhism, while initially developed and practiced in Asia,[25] attempts to bring the western concern with social justice and human rights into the heart of Buddhism.[26] In its radical variant, socially engaged Buddhism stresses the need not just to ameliorate poverty, injustice, and other forms of human suffering through various social reforms, but to challenge and transform root and branch the systemic causes of human suffering.

While I believe that these two trends can and should be fruitfully integrated, it's important to note that secular Buddhism and a radically engaged

Buddhism are distinct trends and are not necessarily linked. One can be a secular Buddhist without being an engaged Buddhist, of any sort. At the same time, one can be a Buddhist committed to radical social change while practicing in a lineage, say of Zen Buddhism, which is not secular. An example of the former is Stephen Batchelor; an example of the latter was Robert Aitken, founder of the Zen Buddhist Diamond Sangha. More recently, key leaders in western Buddhism who have strong roots in traditional lineages have played a leading role in developing a radically engaged form of Buddhism, including Bhikkhu Bodhi, a Theravada Buddhist; and David Loy, a Zen teacher in the Sanbo Zen tradition of Japanese Zen Buddhism.

Secular Buddhists and radically engaged Buddhists embrace Gotama's insights about human suffering and the need for a liberatory path which encompasses meditative practices, ethics, and the development of wisdom. At the same time, both perspectives present challenges to some basic assumptions of mainstream, western Buddhism. On the one hand, secular Buddhists reject or marginalize as irrelevant the transcendent, divine entities and the cosmological realms of the various Asian Buddhisms. More broadly, secular Buddhists critically interrogate the metaphysical or ontological beliefs which are an essential part of the main branches of Buddhism: Theravada, Mahayana, and Vajryana. As Stephen Batchelor has emphasized, Buddhism emerged as an institutionalized religion when Gotama's ethical and pragmatic insights about how to live wisely and ethically in this world gave way to a set of metaphysical beliefs about ultimate reality and absolute truth to which the practitioner must adhere. Secular Buddhists take a different approach; rejecting the ontologization of Buddhism, they attempt to recover Gotama's insights as part of developing a practical philosophy and ethics which is relevant to our contemporary world.[27]

Radically engaged Buddhism critiques another core tenet shared by most western Buddhists – the view that the root cause of social problems is primarily due to individuals' thoughts, emotions, and actions being determined by the three 'poisons': greed, hatred, and delusion. Radically engaged Buddhists agree that the thoughts and actions of individuals who are dominated by the three poisons contribute to social problems such as war, discrimination, and oppression. However, they also emphasize the systemic roots of social ills and the need to transform exploitative and oppressive social institutions.

In what follows, I spell out more fully the critique of mainstream Buddhism advanced by a secular, radically engaged approach. I then offer some ideas on how such a perspective can have a positive impact in transforming the role of the community of Buddhist practitioners, or sangha.

The secular Buddhist critique of mainstream Buddhism

Secular Buddhism is a work in progress, as are many other forms of western Buddhism. The exact border and topography of this trend within Buddhism is thus not fixed at this point and may never be. Attempts to define what secular Buddhism is, as a perspective and practice, are ongoing and far from conclusive. Yet, all self-defined secular Buddhists share at least one thing in common: the rejection of supernatural beings and the cosmology of realms found in Asian Buddhisms, as well as the notion of *karma* linked to literal rebirths. Consistent with this demystification, secular Buddhists see the Buddha not as a god-like figure but as a person – Gotama – who lived in a particular historical and cultural context.

Even as secular Buddhists reject the supernatural dimension of Buddhism, however, there are differences of emphasis and attitude on this issue. At one extreme, are secular Buddhists who are militant atheists. Like Richard Dawkins[28] and others who have sharply criticized Christianity and other theistic religions as being nonsensical and unscientific, these secular Buddhists reject any connection with religion. At the other end, there are secular Buddhists whose position on this matter is agnostic: they assert that we just don't know and perhaps will never know the truth or falsity of claims of transcendent deities or processes not explicable on the basis of natural processes. I find myself more inclined toward the latter position for two reasons. In the first place, a stridently anti-religious form of secular Buddhism can entail an intolerance or unwarranted dismissal of others' spiritual beliefs and practices that reflects a lack of compassion and an attachment to a particular viewpoint. In addition, whether there are transcendent deities and non-naturalistic processes, outside what we now understand to be the naturalistic world, may never be definitively settled. Perhaps, at some point in the future, we will come to conceive of transcendent deities and the natural world in a way that makes the current distinction untenable.

While the rejection of gods, hell realms, devas, and rebirth in another body is an important aspect of secular Buddhism, there is another, equally significant dimension, one strongly emphasized by Stephen Batchelor. In his interpretation of the core insights of the Pali Canon, Batchelor has urged us to see Gotama's teachings as pragmatic, ethical prescriptions for a good and meaningful life, rather than as ontological propositions or 'truths'. From this perspective, Gotama should be seen as a pragmatic healer of human suffering in this world.[29]

Rather than calling on us to escape suffering by accessing a realm of unconditioned freedom and happiness – nirvana – Gotama enjoins us to develop wise, skillful responses to suffering based on the sustained, vigorous cultivation of certain human capacities: self-reflection, mindfulness, and empathy. Our suffering and the solution to our suffering occur within the world of human experience and nature. Batchelor brilliantly applies this approach to his analysis of the doctrine of the Four Noble Truths. Following Ñāṇavīra Thera's[30] interpretation of the early texts, Batchelor retrieves the original ethical thrust of Gotama's teachings by reconstructing the Four Noble Truths as four tasks to think and act in certain ways which promote human flourishing, not statements about the way the world 'is'.[31]

As I noted in the previous chapter, the Four Noble Truths is a foundational element of ancestral Buddhism. The first truth is that life always involves suffering, in both obvious and subtle ways. Even when we have what we want and things seem to be going well, there is often an undercurrent of anxiety and unsatisfactoriness that is inescapable. The second truth is that the cause

Chapter 2 At the Crossroads of Individual and Social Transformation

of this suffering is our craving for good or pleasant experiences, based on a fundamental ignorance of ourselves and reality. However, the third truth is that we can cease craving altogether by understanding the true nature of ourselves and the world. By following the eightfold path, thus living ethically, practicing meditation, and developing wisdom (including understanding the Four Noble Truths), we can gain freedom from suffering just as the Buddha did. This is the fourth truth.

Batchelor argues that it is more appropriate to understand Gotama's core message as composing four interrelated tasks to transform our lives and promote human flourishing in this world:

1) Embrace life;
2) Let reactivity be;
3) See reactivity stop; and
4) Actualize a path.

These four tasks require us to cultivate the mindfulness, compassion, and wisdom needed to flourish and live ethically. A key element of a secular approach is thus the shift from a focus on ultimate truth claims about reality to an emphasis on the pragmatic and ethical dimensions of Gotama's teachings. Batchelor believes that Gotama's original understandings of how to respond to suffering were gradually transformed into an institutionalized religion based on a set of beliefs after he died. Buddhism took a metaphysical turn.

> By adopting the language of truth, Buddhists moved from an engaged agency with the world to the theorizing stance of a detached subject. ... Rather than consider injunctions to guide their ethical actions, they debated the truth of propositions to support their beliefs.[31]

Based on Batchelor's critique of the ontologization of Gotama's pragmatic and ethical insights into forms of dogmatic, metaphysical, and religious beliefs, we can see how Buddhism shares with other religions the notion of an ultimate realm or ground of existence, which John Hick argued is an essential characteristic of all religions.[33] Often, in religious worldviews, the ultimate realm or ground is placed in a binary opposition to the everyday, natural world. Dualisms of this sort are, of course, a common feature of theistic Abrahamic religions: consider the opposing pairs of God-human being, spirit-nature, and heaven-earth found in Christianity. However, the ultimate realm or ground can also be understood non-dualistically, as the necessary condition of all reality, the universal process that integrates the diversity of processes, or as an ineffable, numinous presence that one can encounter in a mystical experience.

All lineages and schools of Buddhism reject the theistic notion that there is a personal God who is the creator of the universe and all of the dualisms consistent with this belief. The rigid separation of nature and spirit – based on an ontological dualism – is thus not a feature of Buddhism either. Yet, it is essential to recognize the various ways in which an ultimate realm is an integral aspect of Buddhism – either in the form of one pole of a duality or, as with Buddhist non-dualistic perspectives, the underlying ground or the unity making possible all forms of existence.

For example, the US-born Theravadan monk Bhikkhu Bodhi has argued that, for Theravada Buddhists, the investigation of our experience reveals a:

> number of critically important dualities with profound implications. ... At the peak of the pairs of opposites stands the duality of the conditioned and Unconditioned: *samsara* as the round of repeated rebirth and death wherein all is impermanent, subject to change, and liable to suffering, and *Nibbana* as the state of final deliverance, the unborn, ageless, and deathless.'[34]

The goal of spiritual practice is precisely the overcoming of greed, hatred, and

Chapter 2 At the Crossroads of Individual and Social Transformation

delusion – the defilements of the mind – and the attainment of a state of full release or freedom from the defilements in Nibbana.

Based on the duality between samsara, the everyday life of suffering, impermanence, conditioned existence, and delusion; and nirvana, the transcendence of samsara, other key dualities can be found in Theravada Buddhism. For example, there is the duality of the samsaric mind and the pure mind. According to Joseph Goldstein, the cultivation of spiritual practice (meditation, ethical behavior, and the development of wisdom) is how the mind is purified and the various defilements are overcome. By purifying the mind, one finds its 'true' nature, which has been covered over by the defilements, for 'the essential nature of our mind and heart is pure'.[35]

Among western Buddhists, the notion of ultimate reality as one pole of a binary opposition is less prominent, however, than non-dualistic conceptions. While Mahayana and Vajrayana Buddhist lineages in the west have, as an integral element, such a non-dualistic view of the ultimate, it can also be found in modernistic versions of Theravada, including the Insight meditation or vipassana tradition. In its non-dualistic variant, the ultimate takes the form of an underlying ground or an immanent unifying process or principle that integrates the diversity of forms in existence.

The Buddhist notion of emptiness (*suññatā* in Pali) plays a central role in non-dualistic conceptions of the ultimate. This notion has its roots in Gotama's experiential insights about the self. In his quest for enlightenment, Gotama recognized that the self is not a fixed, permanent, and independent entity. Rather, when we are mindful of our experiences, we find that the self is constantly changing and that what we call the self is actually more of a process, not a substance or some ahistorical essence. We also see the many ways in which a human being is intrinsically connected with the rest of nature. Understanding that the self is not a permanent, independent entity, we gain insight into the reality of 'not-self' (*anattā* in Pali). However, in asserting that anatta is one of the essential aspects of human experience, Gotama was, according to one plausible interpretation of his teachings, not making a broader metaphysical statement about the nature of the self or of all reality. In fact, when asked, Gotama explicitly refused to declare whether the self existed or not.[36]

Gotama's focus, instead, was how a false view of the self contributes to human suffering. At the same time, he was trying to show the fallacy of the notion of an essential self or *ātman*, the most prominent view of the self in the culture in which he lived. Gotama's view that the self is 'empty' or lacking a substantial essence was subsequently elaborated by some Mahayana schools into the metaphysical view that all beings, objects, and processes lack such an essence. This notion of emptiness as the basic characteristic of ultimate or absolute reality pervades conventional Buddhism.

There are a variety of ways in which emptiness can be related to the relative world of forms. For example, in the development of Mahayana Buddhism, the exact relationship between ultimate reality and the multiplicity of processes, events, objects, and beings in our everyday world has been quite contested.[37] Nonetheless, most mainstream Buddhists do believe that we, as human beings living in the everyday 'relative world', can connect with emptiness or absolute reality. In some Mahayana lineages, direct contact with emptiness is liberation, the experience of nirvana or enlightenment. This is the moment of satori, highlighted in some lineages of Zen Buddhism.[38] However, what is common to many western Buddhist lineages is the notion that human beings can experience emptiness because we all possess 'Buddha-nature'; we all share, at an ultimate level, the ability to connect with the absolute truth of emptiness.[39] In short, 'the world is one within which there is enormous diversity and variety, but it is an integrated whole because it is based on a single process, a single ultimate reality, and shares, in a sense, one Buddha'.[40]

Jack Kornfield – one of the co-founders of Insight meditation in the United States along with Joseph Goldstein and Sharon Salzberg – has incorporated the notion of Buddha Nature into his understanding of the dharma, which is based primarily in Thai and Burmese Theravada teachings and practices. Kornfield argues that, once we understand the sense in which our common view of the self is a form of delusion, we can gain access to a 'true self':

Chapter 2 At the Crossroads of Individual and Social Transformation

Beneath our struggles and beyond any desire to develop self, we can discover our Buddha nature, an inherent fearlessness and connectedness, integrity, and belonging. Like groundwater these essential qualities are our true nature, manifesting whenever we are able to let go of our limited sense of ourselves, our unworthiness, our deficiency, and our longing. The experience of our true self is luminous, sacred, and transforming.[41]

Secular Buddhists agree that we all enjoy the capacity for mindfulness, compassion, and discernment. It allows us to gain some measure of release from greed, hatred, and delusion, and thus to reduce our experience of suffering in the world. But this positive, life-affirming capacity – which Buddhist practice aims to promote – isn't grounded in emptiness or constitute our Buddha nature. Instead, it's part of the complex, multifaceted experience of being human. We have on the one hand, the capacity for mindfulness, compassion, and wisdom, and on the other the capacity for greed, hatred, and delusion which cause our own and others' suffering. From a secular Buddhist viewpoint, there is no absolute reality or ultimate ground for us to discover within ourselves and the world; there is simply the complex experience of limited and conditioned human beings who, in certain contexts, have the potential to make this world a place in which human flourishing and the flourishing of all beings can be maximized.

Our ability to enhance our mindfulness, compassion, and wisdom derives from how we are constituted as conscious, biological beings, and the causes and conditions (including environmental influences) which shape the expression and form of our humanity. We aren't inherently bad or inherently good – an idea often found in monotheistic religions – but complex beings who have developed through the evolutionary process and sociocultural changes.[42] Thus, for Steven Pinker, the psychologist and cognitive scientist, in the course of the evolution of the human species, certain universal capacities and characteristics have developed, constituting our essential human condition. Such capacities and characteristics 'encompass our common pleasures and pains, our common methods of reasoning, and our common vulnerability to folly (not least the desire for revenge).'[43] For Frans de Waal, the universal human capacity for empathy and compassion – so crucial to the Buddhist path – is rooted in the survival advantages accruing from sociality and altruism, which can be found to a lesser extent in other animals. However, in his view, it is our uniquely human cognitive capacities for abstraction, creativity, and learning which allow us, under certain conditions, to move beyond the limited forms of group altruism to envisage and struggle for the flourishing of all human beings.[44]

From this perspective, the path to greater kindness, compassion, and wisdom is not a journey from the relative existence of everyday life to an absolute realm, but a shift from a more painful and contracted existence to a more spacious and fulfilled way of being in the natural and social worlds. Imagine a human being's mind as a house where all the capacities, habits, needs, desires, thoughts, emotions, and sensations of a human being coexist. We suffer, as Gotama recognized, because for much of the time, most of the space of this house is crammed with greed, anger and delusion, and its effects, just as a closet can be filled with unneeded objects. Only a small area – perhaps a tiny attic – has in it those qualities of the mind that foster happiness and fulfillment.

We can then envisage the path and practice of Buddhism as a process in which more and more of the space in this house is filled with skillful thoughts, feelings, and emotions. Greed, anger, and delusion still take up many rooms, but the balance has begun to shift. We can never eliminate greed, anger, or delusion, but we can have a house that is often not dominated by these qualities. Instead, our house is a place in which, increasingly, qualities of the mind that facilitate our happiness and flourishing are present.

In this secular Buddhist metaphor of the human mind, our task is not to make contact with an unconditioned realm – whether viewed as the latter pole of the samsara/nirvana duality or as an underlying ground or unity – but to establish a different relationship between unskillful and skillful qualities of the mind.

Chapter 2 At the Crossroads of Individual and Social Transformation

The radically engaged Buddhist critique of mainstream Buddhism

One of Gotama's core insights is that all things and processes that exist are part of a web of constantly changing causes and conditions. Conditionality is a universal characteristic of all that exists, including human beings. We are not isolated, self-sufficient entities; rather, we are interconnected with and interdependent on all other aspects of existence. This idea contradicts the commonly assumed view of the self. We think that we own or possess our self when, in fact, the self is the sum of the causes and conditions in which the self is embedded. By gaining conceptual and experiential knowledge of the self as conditioned in this respect, we are able, in conjunction with meditative practices and ethical behaviors, to find some release from clinging and thus reduce our experience of suffering.

However, the Buddhist notion that everything that exists is part of a web of constantly changing causes and conditions – the doctrine of dependent origination – is abstract; it does not necessarily provide us with a guide for understanding the specific ways that human beings interact with each other and the complex networks of which we are a part. What are the key causes and conditions that influence human behavior and in what contexts? To what extent is suffering the product of human activity rather than other parts of a complex whole? How and why are social institutions formed and how do they affect human beings? Responding to all these questions is vital if we want to reduce suffering and promote human flourishing. But to answer them we need theoretical tools that the notion of dependent origination cannot provide.

Western Buddhists from all schools and lineages recognize the crucial role that causes and conditions of various kinds have on human beings. From our biological preference for pleasure and aversion to pain, to the vicissitudes of childhood, to the impact of social institutions, the ways in which we are conditioned have a powerful impact on how we think, speak, and act. And yet, the predominant understanding in mainstream Buddhism is that the root cause of the suffering that we experience above and beyond the inevitable physical and emotional pains of life lies within us – namely, the greed, hatred, and delusions that defile our minds. The forms of conditioning that cause us such suffering – even if they occur at a social level – are all ultimately due to the problematic nature of our minds.

It is not surprising that Buddhists see the root cause of suffering as residing in our minds. After all, one of Buddhism's key tenets is that our perceptions and intentions, which are qualities of the mind, are crucial in determining whether we suffer or not. The *Dhammapada*, an anthology of verses from the Pali Canon, famously begins with this assertion of the primary role of the mind:

> All experience is preceded by mind,
> > Led by mind
> > Made by mind.
> Speak or act with a corrupted mind,
> > And suffering follows
> As the wagon wheel follows the hoof of the ox.[45]

Consistent with the notion that mind plays the primary role, most western Buddhists believe that the formation of social institutions and how societies function are based on the qualities of the minds of the individuals in society. As I noted in Chapter 1, theirs is a one-way cause and effect model: the character and quality of social institutions are a reflection of the minds of the human beings that compose them. Because the vast majority of human beings have minds that are caught up in the three poisons, we create social institutions and ideologies that reflect greed, hatred, and delusion. For example, David Loy, a radically engaged Buddhist, has explored the process by which the three poisons are institutionalized in our capitalist economic system (greed), military (hatred), and mass media (delusion).[46]

For conventional Buddhists, then, the basic solution for reducing suffering is for people to change their minds. Those who can release themselves from clinging, hatred and delusion will help to create a world in which peace, calm, and loving compassion are predominant. Even those who are advocates of an engaged Buddhism that emphasizes the need for collective and political action support this point of view. Consider, for example, the comment of perhaps the most famous socially engaged Buddhist, Thich Nhat Hanh, who said:

> We may think of peace as the absence of war, that if the great powers would reduce their weapons arsenals, we could have peace. But if we look deeply into the weapons, we will see our own minds – our own prejudices, fears, and ignorance.[47]

Similarly, when prominent western Buddhist teachers from all the major Buddhist lineages came together in 2014 to form One Earth Sangha in response to the crisis of global warming and climate change, they asserted that the unique Buddhist contribution to responding to this crisis resides in an understanding that the problem of global warming and climate change is ultimately rooted in our mind:

> The dharma informs us ... that craving, aversion, and delusion within the human mind are the root causes of vast human suffering. Just as these mental factors have throughout history led to the oppression, abuse, and exploitation of indigenous peoples and others outside the halls of wealth and power, craving, aversion, and delusion are also the root causes of climate change.[48]

Thus, the remedy lies in cultivating wisdom, ethical conduct, and mindfulness in all human beings.

The problem with this perspective is not that it is wrong but that it is incomplete or partial because it ignores the significant impact of social institutions and class relationships. While *a root cause* of climate change and other social problems is the unskillful ways that the human mind processes experiences and acts, the defilement of the mind is not *the basic cause*. Consequently, the notion that the transformation of individual minds is the most important way to address social problems does not do justice do the complex relationship between individuals and social institutions.

The limitations of Buddhism in this regard require us to incorporate a perspective that better recognizes the complex interaction or dialectic between the individual and society. As I argued in Chapter 1, such a perspective can be found in a non-deterministic, humanistic Marxism which, as a radical social theory and guide to activism, helps us understand the specific causes and conditions that produce human suffering as well the potential for human flourishing. For Marx, these specific causes and conditions are found through an investigation of the real premises of human life: the socio-economic processes and structures by which we produce and reproduce our material existence. According to Marx, the primary dynamic in all the socio-economic systems which have existed after the first hunter-gatherer societies – slave-based, feudal and capitalist ones – has been the conflictual relationship between the majority of people in society and a minority class of wealthy and powerful individuals who own and control the means of production. This class conflict, marked by the exploitation and oppression of the majority by the minority class, is not only a key determinant of society's development but the basic root of social harms and suffering.

Marx insisted that a focus on class conflict and other material conditions does not entail a structural determinism in which human agency has no role. In his *Theses on Feuerbach,* he argued that:

> the materialist doctrine that men are products of circumstances and upbringing, and that, therefore, changed men are products of changed circumstances and changed upbringing, forgets that it is men who change circumstances.[49]

Chapter 2 At the Crossroads of Individual and Social Transformation

Human beings are active, creative beings who transform themselves and their environment through social labor: 'by thus acting on the external world and changing it, he at the same time changes his own nature'.[50]

At any point in time, human activity produces the material conditions of social life. But those material conditions are also 'already existing'; they constitute the specific conditions, beyond our immediate control, that create limits and constraints on human activity. Thus, Marx rejected both the view that social institutions are solely a reflection of the human mind as well as the opposite view that social institutions completely determine human thought and behavior. Instead, he argued that human activity and social conditions mutually presuppose and reciprocally interact with each other, a view he brilliantly articulated in his writing on historical events, such as *The Civil War in France*.[51]

We need to recognize and value the ways in which the transformation of the minds of individuals is crucial to solving social problems and building progressive movements, as Buddhists do. But we must also understand how individual transformation depends on collective activity and a supportive social environment. The causes and conditions that link individual human beings and society are complex and interactive. Cause and effect run not just from the individual to society, but from society to the individual as well.

The structures and processes of neoliberal capitalism have an enormous impact and are exceedingly difficult to change in any more than incremental ways. Today, most of the world's population lives in societies which are dominated by a powerful capitalist class who own and control the means of production. There certainly have been (and will continue to be) successful struggles to make capitalist societies more democratic and socially just, to provide a partial check on the dominance of capitalists over the economy and their influence in the political system. However, given the many ways in which capitalist economic structures are promoted and reinforced – through the education system, work experiences, and the media – it's not surprising that we are socialized to support competition, domination, power over others, and avarice. As a result, our own thinking, speech, and behavior tend to reinforce and reproduce the very same hierarchical and undemocratic social structures.

What kind of change is needed to end the harm to human beings and the ecosystem that neoliberal capitalism causes? Marx argued that the capitalist system must be radically transformed and replaced with a new system if we want to eliminate the exploitation and oppression of people that arises out of the structural power imbalance between the social classes. And he drew attention to the related problem under capitalism of human alienation from ourselves, our labor, the products of our labor, and other people. Further, while Marx wrote little about the damage wrought by capitalism to our environment, his concept of the 'metabolic rift' has been used by contemporary Marxists who are eco-socialists, including Foster and Saito. They explore how capitalism's inherent tendency toward accumulation and growth is a root cause of global warming and climate change.[52]

Only the establishment of a society based on economic and political democracy, as well as an ecologically sustainable model of development, can create the conditions for human freedom and development. Thus, from a radically engaged Buddhist perspective informed by Marx's social theory, ameliorating the negative effects of our socio-economic system is not enough; we need to participate in movements for social change that contribute to systemic changes. For example, the problems of income inequality, unemployment, and poverty – particularly pronounced in the USA – must be addressed not just by redistributing income and wealth to those at the bottom, but by challenging the structural power imbalance between employers and employees which goes to the root of these social problems.

With the benefit of hindsight and painful historical experiences we now know that many obstacles exist to a radical transformation of capitalism and the creation of a democratic socialist society: divisions between workers, the pull of consumerism, the impact of nationalism, and the multifarious ways in which hierarchical and anti-democratic forms of social interaction stubbornly persist. Based on a naïve millenarianism, some Marxists have minimized these factors and assumed that workers will inevitably develop a revolutionary consciousness. They ignore the real obstacles to social transformation, including the human tendencies toward greed, hatred, and delusion that Buddhists have always emphasized. We should, of course, reject such an approach, yet we need to retain Marx's basic idea that, because of their structural position in society, workers can develop the collective power and consciousness to challenge the system. If we understand Marx's view of the potential of workers in this way, we can reject the idea that socialism is inevitable, but still recognize that transformative social change has a very real human and social basis.

For Marx, then, it is the combination of certain uniquely human capacities in interaction with particular causes and conditions – some of which are themselves produced by human beings – that makes social transformation not just desirable, but possible. More precisely put, those human capacities that make possible social transformation can only be actualized within certain social contexts. One example: When workers struggle together for fair treatment on the job, by going on strike for example, they may not only achieve better working conditions and wages in their contract but, as I have witnessed in my almost fifty years of involvement in the labor movement in the United States, the struggle itself may significantly change individual workers. In fact, the capacities for critical intelligence and a strong sense of solidarity between workers – which are necessary conditions for any successful workers' struggle – are most fully developed in the course of collective actions.

But it is not just in labor unions that one can see the positive, transformative impact of collective activity on individuals. Any social movement seeking progressive change and struggling with the status quo will have this effect on individuals to one degree or another. Thus, many people who participated in the American civil rights movement in the early to mid-1960s, were profoundly changed. The white and African American activists who took part in Freedom Summer in Mississippi in 1964 to register to vote and to provide education to African Americans in that segregated, repressive state became part of a 'beloved community', the experience of which shaped their lives in enduring ways.[53]

A radically engaged Buddhism does not in any way devalue the importance of meditation and other spiritual practices that help us to become more calm, wise, and compassionate individuals. Rather, a Buddhist with this perspective understands that the lessening of human suffering and the maximum development of human flourishing require the simultaneous and mutually supporting processes of individual, spiritual transformation and radical, collective action.

Traditional Buddhists, secular Buddhists and radically engaged Buddhism

The dual critique of conventional Buddhism from secular and radically engaged perspectives offers political activists and Buddhist practitioners a valuable way of integrating radical politics with Gotama's core insights. However, as I noted earlier it is possible to combine a radically engaged approach with more traditional forms of Buddhism. Why is it preferable to integrate secular and radically engaged approaches?

Following Karsten Struhl, I believe that a secular approach is a better fit for a life of radical political activism than most forms of ancestral Buddhism.[54] Secular Buddhists reject or put aside beliefs in karma and rebirth which are tied into assumptions about a transcendent, supernatural realm. The focus of secular Buddhism is understanding the natural and social worlds so that we can alleviate suffering and promote flourishing in this life, the only life that we have. To the extent that traditional Buddhists believe that suffering can only be fully overcome if we attain nirvana in a transcendent realm, then they are less likely to see political activism as a core part of their practice. The related notion in traditional Buddhism that we have many lives and can eventually attain nirvana in a future life can also lessen the urgency for political action in this life. If, on the contrary, we recognize that we and other beings only have a finite lifespan, then there will be a strong motivation to make life better by addressing the causes of both individual and social suffering. As Martin Hägglund has pointed out, it is precisely because our own and others' lives are finite that we value this life and seek to improve it:

Chapter 2 At the Crossroads of Individual and Social Transformation

> The sense of finitude – the sense of the ultimate fragility of everything we care about – is at the heart of what I call *secular faith*. To have secular faith is to be devoted to a life that will end, to be dedicated to projects that can fail or break down. ... We all care – for ourselves, for others, for the world, in which we find ourselves – and care is inseparable from the risk of loss. ... Secular faith is committed to persons and projects that may be lost: to make them live *on* for the future. ... The commitment to live on bears the sense of finitude within itself. ... Even when we fight for an ideal that extends far beyond our lives – a political vision for the future, a sustainable legacy for generation to come – we are devoted to a form of life that may cease to be or never be.[55]

In this way, the motivation for and focus of a secular Buddhist approach is firmly rooted in what we can do to reduce suffering and promote flourishing in this life.

Rethinking the role of the sangha

A secular, radically engaged Buddhism calls into question two key tenets of the various schools and lineages of contemporary western Buddhism: the existence of a supernatural dimension of reality and the one-sided emphasis on the mind as the basic source of suffering and release from suffering. This dual critique has important implications for how to rethink core Buddhist concepts and to reimagine how Buddhist practitioners can connect in communities or sanghas with each other. I critically examine core Buddhist concepts and practices in Chapters 4 and 5; here, I offer some thoughts about the role of the sangha.

    The community of practitioners or sangha is one of the 'three jewels' or foundations of Buddhism; the other two are Gotama, who is seen as an exemplar of what Buddhists aspire to achieve in their spiritual path, and the dharma, the body of Buddhist teachings which reflect the way the world is, the natural laws that determine us. For Buddhists, the sangha is an essential part of the path to liberation. Within a sangha, we develop strong relationships with individuals who are walking on the same path. With them, we can talk about the joys and tribulations of practice, discuss and clarify what we hope to achieve, and experience a deep sense of connection. Our spiritual friends in a sangha thus play a crucial role in helping to support our practice. Gotama himself said that having spiritual friends is the 'whole of the holy life' and essential for following the eightfold path.[56]

While all this is true, the sangha can and should be more than just a support for individual practice. For those Buddhists committed to acting and engaging in the world for social change, the sangha can also be a context in which compassion, mindfulness, and equanimity is developed in and through the collective activity of the sangha members. From a radically engaged perspective, such activity should ultimately lead toward a structural transformation of society. However, even efforts to rectify social problems that have less of a transformative impact in the long-run – such as work with prisoners or helping to remove a source of pollution from a community – are valuable in cultivating wholesome qualities among individual sangha members. For that reason, among the various activities that the sangha sponsors and organizes – meditation groups, various courses, and workshops – we need to put more emphasis on the sangha as a participant in movements and campaigns which address climate change, discrimination, and social injustice.

The sangha can also be a place where we develop the capacities for mindfulness and compassion with each other, through relational practices which support these valuable skills. In traditional sanghas, individual practice, particularly in the form of silent meditation, and presentations by teachers are the main forms of activities. In this context, the teacher explains the teachings or key ideas of Buddhism to individual sangha members essentially in a lecture format. In a sangha committed to practitioners' individual transformation and radically engaged activity, relational practices grounded in Insight Dialogue, developed by Gregory Kramer,[57] and the theory and practice of non-violent communication developed by Marshall Rosenberg[58] provide sangha members with the opportunity to develop honest, meaningful relationships as they cultivate the skills of being fully present with each other and speaking truthfully, with kindness and concern. These skills are essential not just for our own development but for political activists committed to radical change.

As we cultivate relational skills in a sangha, we must challenge the habits, ideas, and emotional responses which reinforce systems of oppression, discrimination, and exploitation. For example, institutionalized forms of racism and internalized racism are pervasive in society. While most Buddhist practitioners reject racism, all Buddhists are nonetheless still deeply implicated in and affected by racist structures, habits, and ideas. The sangha should thus be a place where we can help each other understand, explore, and push back against external and internalized racism. An increasing number of sanghas and meditation centers are making this project a core part of their activities and this needs to be expanded as we reimagine the sangha in the 21st century. Two important examples are the anti-racist work being done by the Insight Meditation Community of Washington and the East Bay Meditation Center, both in the United States.

The shift in emphasis from the sangha as a place to develop an individual practice to one in which relational and collective practices are embraced contributes to the democratization of sangha life. This trend is gaining prominence in many western sanghas. In the traditional model of the sangha, inherited from the monastic tradition, there is a hierarchical relationship between teachers and students. In this model, the teacher, as 'the sage on the stage', imparts their wisdom to sangha members, and an elite group of teachers make the key decisions about the sangha. Increasingly, sanghas are moving toward a more horizontal and democratic governance structure based on the equal participation of members, each sharing their knowledge, life experiences and meditative practices. If we as engaged Buddhists want to contribute toward the creation of a democratic, socially just society, then the way we relate to each other within our sanghas must reinforce the contemporary, progressive values of equality, democracy, participation, and inclusiveness, which are the foundation for a just society.

Chapter 3

The 'Truth' of Secular, Radically Engaged Buddhism

A secular, radically engaged approach to Buddhism integrates Gotama's powerful insights about the suffering rooted in the existential-psychological dimension of human experience with a non-dogmatic, humanistic Marxist theory which recognizes how suffering is also caused by social structures and institutions. Bringing these two perspectives into a dialogue can, I believe, inform Buddhist practitioners and political activists. On the one hand, the approach in question enriches the Buddhist path by making it more ethically and socially focused. On the other, political movements can become more sustainable and fruitful by incorporating the Buddhist virtues of mindfulness and compassion into our campaigns and projects.

In Chapters 4 through 6, I use this approach to question key notions in mainstream Buddhism and Left politics. However, in this chapter I need to first address an issue which might seem to be overly theoretical and abstract but which I believe has important practical implications. The issue is: In what ways is a secular, radically engaged perspective 'true'? By exploring what it means to claim that a secular, radically engaged approach is true, I will be highlighting two key points that are essential for developing a perspective and practice which promotes universal flourishing.

First, I will argue that the 'truths' of a secular, radical approach are not universal, absolute, and permanent claims about reality, but rather provisional and limited hypotheses. They are always subject to revision or replacement as we continue to develop our knowledge of the human condition and the world.

This 'fallibilist' notion of truth is crucial if we wish to avoid the dogmatism and sectarianism that often mark debates within the Buddhist community and in Left groups. At the same time, I contend that a secular, radically engaged approach does not give us the 'master key' to understanding human and natural reality; rather than providing some universal framework to understand the world, it offers one valuable approach to improving human and other lives in our contemporary world. We must recognize the limits of any perspective while maintaining a sense of openness and receptivity to other valuable perspectives. At worst, the belief that one's perspective answers all the questions and solves all the problems can lead to grandiosity. More commonly, the negative effect is that we become narrow-minded and overly attached to our own particular perspective. If we wish to contribute to the flourishing of all, we need to understand that a secular, radically engaged approach is true only in a provisional sense and limited in its scope.

Stephen Batchelor on tasks and truths

A good way to begin this discussion is through an examination of Stephen Batchelor's critique of the very notion of truth in traditional Buddhism. As noted in Chapter 2, a key element of his reconstruction of traditional Buddhism is the shift from focusing on truths about reality, to identifying four tasks to be performed in forging a spiritual path which leads to reduced suffering and facilitates human flourishing. These tasks found expression in the original teaching. In highlighting these four interrelated tasks, Batchelor emphasizes the ethical and pragmatic meaning of Gotama's teachings rather than highlighting a set of beliefs which, as expressed in the Four Noble Truths, are presumed to be universal, absolute, and permanent truths. In line with this approach, Batchelor argues that we need to think differently about the very notion of truth. According to him, the meaning of truth for traditional Buddhists is that a statement is true because it corresponds with or reflects an ultimate or objective reality separate from and independent of human beings – hence the expression 'the correspondence theory of truth'. Thus, the First Noble Truth

Chapter 3: **The 'Truth' of Secular, Radically Engaged Buddhism**

– that suffering (*dukkha*) exists – is a statement that claims to correspond with how the world really is. Whatever our subjective experiences and views might be, the First Noble Truth supposedly reflects an objective reality and thus is the only 'correct' view.

Batchelor sees this notion of truth as the correspondence between a statement and objective reality as pervasive in traditional Buddhism and the basis of various Buddhist orthodoxies. Disputes between lineages and schools in Buddhism arise because each lineage or school asserts that they possess the truth about ultimate reality and thus are superior to all others. To avoid this type of pointless conflict and to shift the focus to the practical impact of Gotama's teachings, Batchelor proposes that we adopt a pragmatist theory of truth, which abandons the idea of an ultimate reality that is hidden behind the surface of the everyday world we experience. For Batchelor and other secular Buddhists who adopt this pragmatic position on the meaning of truth, a statement's truthfulness is based on whether it contributes to human flourishing.

In a discussion with Buddhist teachers Christina Feldman and Akincano Mark Weber in a *Tricycle* magazine article, Batchelor expanded on his critique of the correspondence theory of truth by posing a sharp separation between truths and tasks:

> I have a problem with using the word 'truth' at all for what's usually translated as 'the four noble truths'. We'd be much better off if we abandoned that language. As soon as we bring up this notion of truth, we've framed everything within the idea that there is some reality we have to understand: truths are things that you understand or you don't understand. But I don't think that's what the Buddha is trying to do here. He's actually asking us to embrace suffering; he's asking us to let go of craving; he's asking us to see the stopping of craving; and he's asking us to cultivate a way of life, which is the way it's explained in his first sermon, the Dhammacakkappavattana Sutta ('The Setting in Motion of the

Wheel of the Dharma'). And you can say all of that without any reference to the word 'truth' at all.

... as long as you're using the word 'truth,' you're going to be just a whisker away from having a dogmatic view. If we take, for example, the second noble truth as it is usually translated—that 'craving is the origin of suffering'—to me that is a metaphysical statement. You're making a very generalized claim about the nature of reality, and so immediately people get drawn into the discussion: Well, is that really true? What about this? What about that? And down you go into the rabbit hole of theology. Whereas if you frame it as a task, the challenge is: how do I let go of craving? Then you are setting up a whole different doorway to the thoughts and the discussions that follow. Your discussion inevitably will be pragmatic. It won't be, 'Is this true? Is this false? Is this right? Is this wrong?' but, 'How do you get it done?'[59]

In addition to the pragmatic notion of truth, Batchelor asserts that another valid way of understanding truth is to see it in terms of truthfulness, an ethical quality of how we relate to our life. When we claim someone as a true friend, for instance, we use the word in this ethical sense. Truthfulness has to do with how we live, not the truth-value of a statement – that is, its correspondence with a supposed objective reality. Thus, Batchelor has argued that truth is not a theoretical construct but an existential quality; it implies:

...a way of life in which one is true to one's potential ... true to one's values ... and – as a Buddhist – true to the rationale of the dharma... Being "true" in this sense extends beyond how one expresses oneself in words; it has to do with leading a life of integrity, transparency, and honesty in everything one does.[60]

Chapter 3: **The 'Truth' of Secular, Radically Engaged Buddhism**

Tasks versus truths?

In emphasizing the centrality of tasks in the dharmic path and advocating a pragmatic theory of truth, I believe that Batchelor has not adequately addressed a legitimate concern about the role and meaning of truth. Whether or not it was his conscious intention to do so, it appears that he has set up an unhelpful dichotomy between truths and tasks for dharma practitioners. One either believes in certain fundamental truths or one engages in certain tasks. Traditional Buddhism is belief/truth-based and secular Buddhism is task-based.

This is an unhelpful dichotomy. In fact, truths and tasks are inescapably connected. Thus, the four tasks presuppose a whole set of beliefs and understandings about human experience and the world, including:

- ☆ Life, as experienced by human beings, has an inescapably tragic dimension but also has a joyful/pleasant dimension.
- ☆ Human beings tend to be reactive in relation to our difficult inner and outer experiences because of biologically evolved characteristics and social conditioning.
- ☆ Such reactivity creates 'surplus' suffering beyond the emotional and physical pains that are inevitable in life, and thus hinders one's ability to flourish as a human being.
- ☆ By embracing life in all its complexity and learning how to be less reactive, we can live more fulfilling and satisfactory lives – i.e., we can flourish as human beings.
- ☆ We have the ability as human beings to cultivate emotional and intellectual capacities which reduce our reactivity.
- ☆ Although we are inescapably connected to the web of causes and conditions that constitute natural existence, our capacity to 'unhook' from reactivity through mindfulness, wisdom, and compassion allows us to have 'nirvanic' moments in which reactivity is absent.
- ☆ Personal transformation through engaging in the four tasks is not just

for the purpose of individual transformation but is inextricably linked to the creation of a more just society in which all human beings enjoy the possibility of flourishing.

These statements in turn are based on views about the way the world is at its deepest level and most general form (ontology), what is a just society (political philosophy), the virtues that contribute to human flourishing (ethics), the relationship between the individual and society (sociology), and the essential or natural capacities and characteristics of human beings (psychology, philosophy). In short, the four tasks are crucially dependent on a whole series of beliefs, understandings, and theories which justify the value of this approach.

When we engage in any task as human beings, as self-conscious, sentient, and embodied animals, we always do so on the basis of implicit or explicit beliefs underpinning our practice. Even the most basic, rote tasks have this characteristic. And those beliefs represent a type of truth claim; they are statements about the way human beings and the world are as well as could be. So, it appears that tasks can never be separated from claims about the nature of human beings and the world – in short, truth claims. The key question is: In terms of the general relationship between tasks and truths, what is the nature of these truth claims?

Capital T Truths and small t truths

Batchelor is right to critique the notion of a certain kind of truth claim – i.e., metaphysical truths, or truth claims about an ultimate reality – in his secular approach to the dharma. In the first place, debates over metaphysical truths tend to be tautological; the criteria used to judge whether a claim about ultimate reality is correct depend on assumptions that underlie that same account. Thus, there is no independent standard that we can use to judge which account of ultimate reality is correct. Further, in the context of Buddhism, the debate over metaphysical truths presupposes a notion that is absent from Gotama's own teachings: the two truths doctrine. This is the notion that there are two kinds of

Chapter 3: **The 'Truth' of Secular, Radically Engaged Buddhism**

truth: conventional or relative truths which correspond to our everyday experiences and our practical need to function in the world; and absolute truths which correspond with the ultimate nature of reality. Batchelor argues that there is no basis in the original teachings of Gotama for the two truths doctrine, and that it conflicts with the whole thrust of his message. The two truths doctrine takes us away from the essential task at hand – the reduction of suffering.[61]

In The Shorter Discourse to Mālunkyāputta[62] Gotama refused to take a stand on the metaphysical issues of his day – whether the world is eternal, the relationship of the soul to the body, and so on – primarily for this reason. He asserted that the debate over metaphysical issues is sterile and irrelevant insofar as it does not help us to gain freedom from suffering. Just as important, as Batchelor points out, the assertion of metaphysical truths is both the cause and effect of unresolvable divisions and conflicts within Buddhism. Each lineage or school has their own account of ultimate reality, and each group deems its own metaphysical truths to be superior to other accounts. The tendency for Buddhists to fall prey to 'superiority conceits' of various types (a subject which Bhikkhu Analayo has explored in depth),[63] arises in part from the habit of reducing Buddhism to a set of metaphysical truths.

For these reasons, making adherence to metaphysical truths the basis of the dharmic path is deeply problematic. But does that mean that we need to reject entirely the idea of truth as the correspondence between a statement expressing a belief or understanding of the world and the way things are?

The answer is, no, provided that we distinguish between two sorts of truth claims. The truth claims of traditional Buddhism (and other religions) assert a correspondence between certain core beliefs – e.g., 'Craving, rooted in the delusion of a separate self, is the cause of suffering.' – and a pre-existent, objective, and ultimate reality. Such claims are universal, absolute, and permanent. Let us call these truth claims with a capital T, Truths. In contrast, there are truth claims which are more modest in nature; they assert a correspondence between statements and our current, fallible understandings and experiences of the world. Statements about the world are, like scientific hypotheses, always provisional and subject to refutation or revision in the future. Truth claims based on this type of correspondence are small t truths.

Consider the following statement which is presupposed in the four tasks: Human beings have the tendency to crave but also the capacity to be mindful and compassionate. This is a statement or hypothesis about how we, as human beings, are constituted and function in the world. When we speak of the truth of this statement in the small t sense, we mean that, based on what we currently know about human beings and the natural world, this statement reflects the way things are. It is an accurate representation of what exists as we experience and know it now. However, we may develop new understandings of human beings and the world that will require us to revise this statement. We need to keep an open mind; this issue has not been definitively settled for all time.

If we think of the four tasks as not just specific actions to take but also as entailing a set of hypotheses about how to create a flourishing human life, then truth is an important component of the four tasks. When we engage with these tasks, we need to assess the results of our efforts in achieving the stated, overall objective of human flourishing. As Gotama said repeatedly, to make progress in the dharmic path, we should not believe something based on someone else's view, traditional doctrines, and even his own words. Instead, he said it was essential have a direct experience of the path; the dharma is something that each person needs to come and see – *ehipassiko* – for themselves. We need to experience the process and results of the various aspects of the path to know if they actually contribute to our own and others' flourishing.

Crucially, the results of our efforts to engage with the four tasks are not predetermined; they are affected by a variety of causes and conditions. At the same time, our understanding of human beings and the natural world continues to develop as we gain new knowledge in various fields. Thus, the 'truth' of the four tasks will always be conditional and provisional. The correspondence between the hypotheses contained in the fourfold task and the inferred results (mindfulness, compassion, a socially just society) will always be subject to future experiences and new ways of understanding ourselves and the world.

Chapter 3: **The 'Truth' of Secular, Radically Engaged Buddhism**

Tasks and truths

By insisting that Gotama's teachings are most fruitfully read from a pragmatic and ethical lens, Batchelor has correctly pointed out the problems with Buddhism becoming a religion based on metaphysical truths – i.e., Truths. He is also right to assert that the truth value of the four tasks and other key teachings is based on whether it promotes human flourishing, not some correspondence with an ultimate reality. Yet, as I have argued, the truth value of the four tasks (and the beliefs and theories which underlie it) is also due to its correspondence with the way things are, as we currently experience and understand this reality. Rather than counterposing tasks to truths, as Batchelor does, we ought to see the tasks and small t truths of the four tasks as being inescapably connected. The pragmatic view that the truth value of the four tasks resides in their facilitating human flourishing cannot be separated from the notion that the four tasks are true because they correspond with the way things are. If the four tasks work in a pragmatic way, it is because the beliefs and perspectives underlying them are true in that they correspond with what exists in the natural and social worlds.

When we engage in the four tasks, we are not just thinking, speaking, and acting in certain ways in performance of the tasks. We do so because we have certain views about ourselves and the world which we believe to be valuable and important truths; and those truths are borne out by our experiences. The difference between this secular approach and traditional Buddhism is that our focus is reducing suffering and facilitating human flourishing in this world, not the attainment of permanent release from suffering to achieve nirvana, and that we understand these truths to be conditional and provisional. We engage in the four tasks with a deep commitment to our beliefs – which we believe to be true – but also with a sense of intellectual humility and a willingness to embrace uncertainty. The secular dharmic path challenges us to assess constantly both our tasks and the truths on which they are based.

This may all seem to be a bit of a conceptual quibble about the meaning of truth claims. Why insist on the value of a particular notion of truth as correspondence in this context? This is the concern that Winton Higgins, a secular Buddhist from Australia, has raised in response to my analysis of truths and tasks. Higgins believes that the sharp distinction between metaphysical truths and pragmatic tasks found in Stephen's approach is essential because it poses the choice between acceptance of traditional Buddhist orthodoxy and engaging with the pragmatic and ethical tasks laid out by Gotama. He contends that my perspective – which is based on connecting small t truths with pragmatic tasks – obscures this choice.

> A lot more than a conceptual dichotomy is in play here. 'Truths' and 'tasks' stand for divergent paths and responses to the human condition. It's not an epistemological issue about the status of truth – it's an existential one about how we should live and practise. I'm afraid dharma practitioners do have to choose: they can't wish-wash over the truths/tasks distinction.[64]

While I recognize Higgins's concern, the rejection of any notion of truth can create unnecessary confusion for those who are exploring a secular dharmic path. Truth as correspondence is a commonsense notion; for many people, it defines what truth is. So, it is not surprising that practitioners learning about secular Buddhism often express unease about the sharp distinction between truths (negative) and tasks (positive) in Batchelor's writings. They have wondered why they must choose between the two – truths or tasks. If secular Buddhism has important things to say about how we live and understand the world, how can secular Buddhism not involve truths? On a practical, pedagogical level, then, it makes no sense to exclude any notion of truth from a secular dharma.

There is a second practical reason for insisting on the distinction between Big T Truths and small t truths. In rejecting metaphysical truths as the basis of Buddhist orthodoxy, Batchelor rightly emphasizes the role of doubt and uncertainty on the dharmic path. This is one of the most important and valuable elements of his approach. The notion of small t truths is entirely

Chapter 3: The 'Truth' of Secular, Radically Engaged Buddhism

consistent with and supports this key point. If truth is always provisional and conditional, then we need to keep an open mind, recognizing that there is no final or absolute truth. Like a scientist who is always aware that the latest discoveries and theories can be challenged and overturned by new research, the secular dharma practitioner is not attached to their current understandings and experiences. While deeply committed to the secular dharma project, she/he is aware that they may be revised based on new discoveries.

Finally, if we want to refine and further develop a secular Buddhist approach, then we need to clarify what our beliefs and perspectives are and probe their truth-value. For example, secular Buddhists believe that we have the tendency to attach (negatively or positively) to our experiences, but also the capacity to be mindful and compassionate. What does that mean? Is this belief consistent with the findings of contemporary science? Which of these aspects of humanity is dominant, and under what circumstances? All these questions and many more need to underpin an ongoing assessment of, and reflection on, a secular dharmic path. A recognition that secular Buddhism involves truth claims helps us to keep in mind the necessity of that process of examination and inquiry.

Avoiding the superiority conceit: two guardrails

The truths of a secular, radically engaged Buddhism are thus limited and provisional; they are not metaphysical claims, universal and absolute propositions about reality. This perspective also does not provide a master key to explaining all reality. It turns its back on any so-called theory of everything. And finally, a secular, radically engaged approach will not provide an appropriate path for all people. It is not the one, right way which all people need to follow. Yet I strongly believe that a secular, radically engaged perspective does offer us important insights and understandings about the human condition and the world, and how we can contribute to human flourishing. In short, in this book I aim to integrate a deep sense of theoretical humility with passionate advocacy for a secular, radically engaged approach.

Both Buddhist and Left political circles exhibit the pervasive problem of a lack of theoretical humility. Bhikkhu Analayo has discussed this issue in the context of the development of Buddhism, focusing on the ways in which important groups and lineages within Buddhism have asserted that their approach and perspective are uniquely correct – the so-called superiority conceit – and criticized other approaches as being inferior. Analayo explains how both Theravada and Mahayana Buddhists assert that their particular version of Buddhism is the true one; and that the beliefs and practices of other lineages are inferior or just plain wrong. Analayo demonstrates that these claims are fundamentally mistaken because they're based on various distortions and misinterpretations.[65]

However, his contention that secular Buddhism, as advocated by Stephen Batchelor, likewise suffers from a superiority conceit is much less persuasive. Batchelor has never claimed that his interpretation of Gotama's teachings is superior to others. Moreover, secular Buddhists by and large reject the notion that their perspective represents a pure form of Buddhism, and that all other versions of Buddhism are deficient. In fact, among secular Buddhists, there is a refreshing sense of openness to various perspectives.

Nevertheless, the tendency to take on a superiority conceit is very strong. In the interests of promoting a culture of respect and dialogue, I offer two propositions in the context of Buddhism which provide us with guardrails to avoid developing a superiority conceit.

☆ Secular, radically engaged Buddhism does not constitute the 'correct' way of understanding Gotama's teachings in comparison to other approaches, including traditional lineages of Buddhism. Based on our values, interests and needs, secular, radically engaged Buddhists engage in a specific way with the texts and traditions of Buddhism, as do many other approaches. Secular, radically engaged Buddhism is one among a variety of legitimate approaches; it does not represent the 'pure' or 'right' way. Like other individuals and movements who have offered us powerful, complex, and deep ways of understanding and acting in the world, Gotama's teachings can and will foster a variety of interpretations and applications.

☆ While the dharma provides valuable insights and practices, neither a secular, radically engaged nor a conventional version of Buddhism gives us a master key for understanding all the salient processes and events of individual experiences and social life. Because Gotama's teachings are limited in some important respects, we need other theories and perspectives to complement, supplement, and/or revamp core Buddhist ideas.

Guardrail #1
There is no one, correct interpretation of Gotama's teachings

Let's start with what virtually all Buddhist practitioners can agree with. First, Gotama's teachings offer profound insights about human existence, in particular, the ways in which our tendency to attach to and fundamentally misunderstand our experiences cause us various forms of discontent, dis-ease, and suffering. In addition, Gotama provided us with an overall path which integrates meditation, wisdom, and ethics for transforming our lives and substantially reducing suffering. Third, his analysis of the cause of suffering and his prescriptions for remedying suffering are not limited to a subset of human beings but apply to all humans; his teachings are universal. And finally, there is also agreement on more specific points as well: the conditioned and impermanent nature of all human experience; the interconnectedness of beings, events, and objects within nature; the need to move away from an ego-centric mode of being; and the crucial value of emotional tones or attitudes which facilitate a more connected, less ego-centered stance – loving kindness, compassion, sympathetic joy, and equanimity.

So, as I noted in Chapter 1, there is an agreed-upon core to Gotama's teachings. Interpretations inconsistent with the dharmic tradition can be labelled as incorrect or illegitimate. Thus, to pose the issue in an outlandish way, if someone were to say that Gotama supported a lifestyle based on crass materialism, the satisfaction of immediate desires, and doing harm to others to achieve our own goals, then that interpretation would clearly contradict the dharma. Of course, disputes within Buddhism over interpreting Gotama's teachings are not as easily resolved as that. They have to do with how people, in various contexts and time periods, and with different interests and needs, have engaged with the core teachings – as we have come to know them in various texts and stories. If an interpretation or perspective about Gotama's teachings falls within the core set of ideas, such interpretation is as legitimate as any other that accepts these core ideas.

Because Gotama's teachings and prescriptions for living a good life have an immense depth, richness, and complexity, it is not surprising that a wide variety of interpretations, perspectives, and practices based on those teachings has arisen. It is precisely because Gotama offered us such an innovative and powerful vision of human experience that for over 2,500 years people in many different cultures have sought to understand and make these teachings relevant in their own lives. At any one time and within any culture, there are always divergent views about what counts as the most useful or best interpretation. The continuing debate over how to interpret early Buddhist texts is a good example.

Bhikkhu Analayo is one of the most prolific and insightful interpreters of early Buddhist texts, including the Pali Canon. We can appreciate and respect Analayo's scholarship, his superb analysis of the Pali Canon and other key texts. At the same time, we should also note that his approach not only includes the guidelines appropriate for a rigorous philological examination of texts, but is shaped by an approach which is rooted in Theravada Buddhism. He is attempting to explain and make relevant for the contemporary world a version of Buddhism which validates the traditional Theravadan notions of karma, rebirth, and the centrality of monastic life to the path of complete liberation from suffering.

On the other hand, Stephen Batchelor is approaching the same texts with a different purpose. He engages with the same early texts in order to develop a

Chapter 3: **The 'Truth' of Secular, Radically Engaged Buddhism**

perspective which promotes individual transformation in lay life, and a broader culture of awakening in relation to the needs, values, and perspectives of our contemporary society. He leaves to one side notions like rebirth and karma, which are foundational to ancestral Asian forms of Buddhism. Instead, he uncovers connections between Gotama's teachings and the challenges that we face today. He does so by interpreting Gotama through an ethical, pragmatic, and phenomenological lens. His approach isn't superior to Analayo's; it is simply different.

The work of any innovative thinker who develops a new and powerful perspective that addresses the human condition inspires the same diversity of interpretations as Gotama's teachings. As someone committed to democratic socialism and a progressive labor movement, I have explored Marxist and radical political theory in depth over the years. Just as the meaning and implications of Gotama's teachings are vigorously contested, interpretations and uses of Marx's writings have widely varied. Marx's legacy has always been disputed, and to such an extent that any two perspectives that claim to be Marxist can vary so much as to look like polar opposites. Marx himself was concerned about the distortion of his ideas. In a letter to Bernstein, Engels quoted Marx as saying that 'what is certain is that I myself am not a Marxist.'[66]

People in different cultures and time periods question and engage with any new, fecund theory or perspective that addresses an essential aspect of human life as they seek to understand and effect positive changes in their lives. When secular, radically engaged Buddhists interpret Gotama's teachings in a particular way, we are engaging in a practice as old as human culture itself.

Guardrail #2
Secular and traditional versions of Buddhism don't have all the answers

No theory or perspective can provide us with a master key to explain the totality of life and provide solutions to all the problems and dilemmas that we encounter. The reason is quite simple. Life is just too complex, uncertain, and changing to expect that one theory or perspective can provide us with all the answers. No one has yet proposed a plausible theory of everything. That's true of secular, radically engaged Buddhism, ancestral forms of Buddhism, Marxism, Freudianism, evolutionary theory, and every other important perspective.

I'm not arguing, as Lyotard and other postmodernists have, that any so-called universal narrative is suspect simply because it presupposes that there are objective facts and general truths which the perspective reveals.[67] Nor am I claiming that all perspectives are just forms of discourse and our assessment of perspectives is so completely relativistic that we can't distinguish between better or worse perspectives. My point is quite different. The fact that a perspective yields multiple interpretations reveals that it connects strongly with our human lives, with the reality of our experience. Such a perspective is thus more valuable than those perspectives which die out or no longer attract interest.

Buddhism certainly fits in the category of perspectives that have captured important aspects of our lives. Buddhism, however, whether in a traditional or secular form, is incomplete in some important ways. Gotama's teachings arose out of the particular conditions and culture in which he lived. The issues and disputes that were most important for Gotama at that time do not neatly correspond to the challenges that we face today. From our contemporary perspective, his core teachings call for restatement in twenty-first century terms, complemented by modern sources of knowledge about human affairs.

Based on my own experience, values, and perspectives, here are some key areas where I believe Gotama's insights and teachings need to be complemented, supplemented, and/or revamped by other perspectives:

☆ While Gotama's understanding of our mind-heart-body provides the basis for a Buddhist psychology which has been enormously helpful in leading to various mindfulness-based treatment modalities for emotional and mental distress, the teachings lack a depth psychology which identifies how unconscious aspects of the mind play a key role

Chapter 3: **The 'Truth' of Secular, Radically Engaged Buddhism**

in psychological development, distress, and treatment.
☆ While Buddhist teachings rightfully emphasize how the three 'poisons' of greed, hatred, and delusion in individuals have a negative social impact, Buddhism fails to recognize that exploitative and oppressive social structures are not just the result of the unskillful thoughts and actions of individuals but are a relatively autonomous source of suffering. There is a mutually interactive or dialectical connection between individual and social dukkha, as well as individual flourishing and social transformation.
☆ While Gotama's teachings and the earliest sanghas represented a departure from traditional notions of social caste and gender, conventional Buddhist institutions are marred by misogyny and a teacher-centric model which conflicts with contemporary values of equality, inclusion, democracy, and diversity.
☆ While Gotama correctly understood the pitfalls of attachment and craving, the prescription of renunciation as an antidote to craving has led to a tendency to deny the value of the body, sensuous experience and close relationships, thus detracting from human flourishing as we would understand it today.

Of course, this is just a partial list. Others will identify additional areas in which they find Buddhist teachings need updating and complementing. The list illustrates a basic point: while we are justified in believing that Buddhism makes a crucial contribution to individual and social well-being, so do other perspectives and practices. Only fundamentalists cleave to just one perspective. We need to see Buddhism as one of a number of perspectives and practices that, in a fruitful conversation with each other, can help us to address the challenges that we face today.

Theoretical humility and passionate advocacy

A strong sense of theoretical humility based on the recognition of the limited and provisional nature of the truths of a secular, radically engaged approach does not entail a wishy-washy orientation toward its core teachings. Unfortunately, some Buddhists assume that taking a strong position on an issue, feeling passionate about one's views, somehow negates the state of non-attachment needed to avoid falling into the pitfall of the superiority conceit. Even worse, it is assumed that passionate commitment leads to rancorous disputes, and ultimately to harm and violence to adherents of different views.

Certainly, if in our passionate support for a perspective, we believe that only our perspective has the correct and true answers, then serious problems are likely to arise in theory and practice, including dogmatism and the superiority conceit. However, if we recognize the limits and provisional nature of our perspective, we can still believe strongly and wholeheartedly that a secular, radically engaged approach to the dharma is a valuable perspective which can have a transformative impact on our lives and contribute to social change. We can confidently assert that position with others.

Yet, to avoid the tendency to see our perspective as being superior, we need to respect these two guardrails. They encourage us to hold our views with humility and good grace. They also give us a broader frame within which to situate our advocacy of a secular, radically engaged Buddhism, or any other perspective.

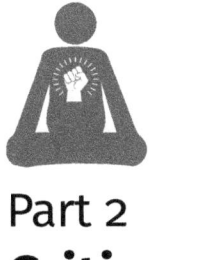

Part 2
Critique

Chapter 4
The Role and Goal of Meditation

In the countries of the Global North, meditation and Buddhism are virtually synonymous. Most so-called convert Buddhists – i.e., individuals who did not grow up in a culture in which Buddhism was prominent and who embraced Buddhism as adults – have engaged with Buddhism as part of developing a meditation practice. This was certainly the case with me. I first started to meditate in 2010 at the urging of my wife, Sharon, who had some experience with the Insight meditation tradition and had read books by two of that tradition's most prominent teachers, Joseph Goldstein and Jack Kornfield. I was going through a rough time due to work-related stress and found that my usual exercise routines and other forms of relaxation were not enough to reduce the pervasive anxiety I was experiencing. Within a short period of time, I found that mindfulness meditation was very helpful in reducing my level of anxiety.

Having experienced the beneficial effects of meditation, I began to explore the Buddhist perspectives and ideas underlying the practice. My wife and I connected with a local Insight meditation center and I felt at home among practitioners who were committed to a dharma practice that was oriented toward mindfulness and compassion without the rituals and cultural trappings that are part of many ancestral forms of Buddhism.

While ethical action, compassion, and generosity were certainly emphasized by the teachers at this center and then at the retreats we attended at the Insight Meditation Society in Barre, Massachusetts, the cornerstone of the practice was clearly meditation. In their dharma talks and instructions for meditation practice, the teachers conveyed to us that it was through individual, silent meditation that we could gain the crucial experiential insights that would lead to a peaceful, less stress-filled life. The ultimate goal of this meditation-centered practice was to achieve a kind of transformation of one's understanding and way of being in the world. The exact nature of this transformation and to what extent it could be achieved was a bit fuzzy, however. Some teachers de-emphasized talk of nirvana as the final goal of meditation, in the sense of a complete and permanent liberation from suffering; they focused on the impact of practice on this life. Other teachers did assert that the path to achieving nirvana was an essential aspect of practice, even if fully experiencing nirvana was quite difficult.

To develop the meditative skills needed for such a radical transformation, all the teachers asserted that we need to overcome hard-wired tendencies in human beings which lead us astray and away from real happiness. Humans seek and want to hold on to pleasant experiences, while we push away and are averse to unpleasant experiences. The problem is that because our built-in desire for pleasant experiences can never be fully or permanently satisfied, we are bound to be frustrated and suffer. At the same time, this ceaseless appetite (greed) for pleasant experiences is underpinned by a fundamental delusion about ourselves. Each person thinks of themselves as an 'I' who possesses a solid, substantial self; this I is the center and source of all our experiences. But the notion of an I, a substantial self, is a hard-wired delusion which is the basis for and facilitates our egotistic grasping at pleasant experiences. Both the human tendency toward what they referred to as greed and aversion, and a delusory notion of the self are products of human evolution and then are reinforced by psychological and social conditioning.

Making progress in meditation requires us to overcome these natural tendencies and various forms of conditioning. Our first task in meditation is to cultivate the ability to become calm and tranquil so we are no longer dominated by the frantic motions of a distracted, overexcited 'monkey mind' driven by greed and aversion. Once we are in a calmer state, we learn how to engage with

Chapter 4: The Role and Goal of Meditation

our experiences, whether pleasant, unpleasant, or neutral, in a non-attached way. Through this process of mindful engagement, we can gain insight into the so-called three marks of existence: that change or impermanence characterizes all existence; that life is often inescapably painful and distressing in various ways; and that the self is not a substantial, separate entity, but rather a process in which different experiential components come together sequentially based on particular 'causes and conditions'. By learning how to gain calm and tranquility, and then to mindfully experience these three marks, we can free ourselves from the pain and suffering and attain a true understanding of reality. (Some teachers, however, have proposed the reverse relationship between calm and insight, asserting that insight is the basis for calm.)

While my initiation into meditation and Buddhism was through Insight meditation, other lineages and schools of traditional Buddhism in the west, including Zen Buddhism and Tibetan Buddhism, share a similar view about the primacy of meditation and its ultimate goal. There are differences of emphasis of course. Theravada Buddhists, of which Insight meditation is one expression, tend to see progress in meditation practice as a path marked by an increasingly deep cultivation of mental skills, a strict adherence to ethics, and gains in the depth of understanding of the foundational notions of Buddhism: the Four Noble Truths, conditionality, and the three marks of existence. At a certain point, it is then possible to attain 'penetrative wisdom', the breakthrough moment that *leads to* nirvana, the complete and permanent cessation of suffering.

On the other hand, Mahayana Buddhists, including Zen and Tibetan Buddhists, tend to emphasize not the series of steps or *path to* nirvana, but an *opening toward* nirvana that is already present. In this sense, Mahayana Buddhist meditation is not about the striving to access the unconditioned, something beyond what we experience day to day. Rather, the goal is to achieve a kind of receptivity or openness to nirvana, which is understood as an ultimate reality already present in the world.

However progress or success in meditation practice is understood, another commonality among traditional Buddhists is the emphasis on the value of meditation retreats, particularly in a residential setting, as the most propitious way to develop meditative skills. Residential retreats typically occur in quiet and serene locations far from urban areas. The main activity at retreats is structured periods of individual, silent meditation which are guided by meditation teachers and range from several days to several months. Except for brief periods of time, silence is maintained throughout the retreat to avoid external stimulation and to encourage the retreatants to focus solely on cultivating mindfulness and concentration during their waking hours. In this context, it is argued, practitioners develop the capacity both to concentrate and collect the mind and to gain insight into core realities of our human experience. By removing the typical stimuli of daily life – smart phones, computers, and other electronic technologies; phone and personal communication with others; work, and the various modes of distraction and amusement – we can become more continually aware of what one is experiencing and how the mind habitually reacts to such experiences with clinging (craving and/or aversion) and delusion. When we can focus more continually on sensations, feelings, and thoughts, the mind not only begins to settle down and become calmer, but we can grasp more deeply the insubstantial, impermanent, and unsatisfactory aspects of our experience. Through this intense process, meditative skills are cultivated and progress along the path becomes possible. And perhaps, nirvana can come into view and be touched...

David McMahan on the social imaginary of meditation

The perspective on the role and goal of meditation which I've described above remains the predominant one among contemporary Buddhists. As I moved toward a secular, radically engaged approach, I began to question some of the ideas underlying this view. While I believe that meditation practice is extremely valuable and that meditation retreats can help to develop meditative skills, it became increasingly apparent to me that certain assumptions about the role and goal of meditation are faulty. David McMahan's critical analysis of

Chapter 4: The Role and Goal of Meditation

what he calls the 'standard version' of meditation insightfully highlights these problematic assumptions and strongly resonates with my own experiences. McMahan identifies the following questionable notions of the standard version: an emphasis on meditation as an individual, private experience; a claim that meditation allows us to gain direct access to the way reality 'really' is, to the 'Truth' in some ultimate sense, as part of the process of achieving nirvana; and finally, that meditation is a kind of scientific technique for observing the mind.[68]

While McMahan believes that the standard version of meditation is deeply problematic, he acknowledges the value that meditation has for many people. His concern is that the standard version is essentially ahistorical; it fails to recognize that the changing social and cultural contexts in which meditation has been practiced fundamentally shape the process, meaning, and purpose of meditation. To understand meditation practice today, we thus need to recognize the historical changes in our society and culture which have transformed meditation practice since Gotama's teachings on meditation in the Satipaṭṭhāna Sutta[69] and other discourses. Specifically, we need to recognize that the standard version of meditation combines *certain* aspects of early Buddhism and Zen Buddhism with key elements in contemporary thought and society, including an emphasis on the isolated individual as the source of knowledge and experience:

> Meditation has ... been adapted to the post-Enlightenment view of the autonomous individual for whom being with others, being in society, and living in concert with social norms is considered a potential imposition on the individual's freedom. Meditation is thus framed as the ultimate individualistic practice of the singular mind gazing at itself and discerning the truth of things in isolation.[70]

McMahan criticizes the notion that 'meditation breaks through to a pristine, unmediated, unambiguous, and Universal Truth beyond the 'trappings of particular religions and all culturally informed assumptions, biases, and conditioning – and that all meditative traditions culminate in the Truth'.[71] In his view, the process, meaning, and ultimate objectives of meditation are always based on and embedded in particular cultural and social forms:

> ... meditation cannot make any sense without a rich surrounding context of ideas, social practices, cultural orientations, and ethical commitments. Such contexts inform not only practitioners' explicit understanding of what they are doing, but also their pretheoretical, tacit, implicit orientations, and even the experiences the practices generate.[72]

The surrounding context within which meditation has meaning and functions is 'a social imaginary ... a social and cultural context in which people live and make sense of their lives'.[73] The social imaginary that shapes contemporary meditation practices includes certain cultural influences and perspectives that have acted as magnets to incorporate aspects of early Buddhist and Zen Buddhist meditation into a new, contemporary version of meditation: Romanticism, Transcendentalism, scientific rationalism, Christianity, and psychology. According to McMahan, these are all important elements in the emergence and development of secular, liberal democratic societies, and they constitute a social imaginary which has profoundly shaped how we view and practice meditation today.

> ... this combination of Enlightenment rationalism, romanticism, social psychology, and Orientalism with selected elements of Buddhist doctrine helped generate new individualistic, secularized versions of meditation that aspired to a kind of interior freedom that wove together western liberal conceptions of personal autonomy and ethical agency with Buddhist conceptions of freedom and liberation. It envisioned a kind

of interior invulnerability and security, freedom from social norms and conditioning—an Inner Citadel that at once provided a respite from world chaos as well as the conditions of ethical agency.[74]

In the context of the social imaginary of secularism and liberalism that marks our contemporary society, there is a set of values which guides contemporary meditation: an ethic of the *appreciation* of life, an ethic of *authenticity*, an ethic of *autonomy*, and an ethic of *interdependence*. While the first three ethics are based on the notion of meditation as an exploration of the individual's interior, these ethics are in tension with the fourth component of contemporary meditation, an ethic of interdependence, which highlights the 'inevitable embeddedness of any meditator in a social, cultural, and political context'[75] and the need for meditators to bring a compassionate concern for others into their practice.

We see this tension play out in the debate about the role of mindfulness in society. For many people, mindfulness meditation offers the relief of individual suffering, de-stressing, and gaining the ability to function better amidst the challenges of everyday life. Others have critiqued this approach as overly individualistic and apolitical. For example, socially engaged Buddhists emphasize that mindfulness needs to become an integral part of projects and movements to challenge forms of exploitation, discrimination, and oppression in society. As McMahan notes,

> There is, therefore, a tension between two poles of interpretation of modern, secular mindfulness practices: at one pole is mindfulness as a private matter, a matter of personal experience and psychological health or instrumental efficiency; on the other is mindfulness as an awakening to a more urgent sense of connectedness with others, which in turn may foster particular ethical sensibilities.[76]

McMahan's core idea that meditation is fruitfully understood as an embodied practice which occurs within particular social and cultural contexts is valuable and important. There is no right or wrong way to meditate, nor does meditation practice allow us to grasp reality as it really is – as the Truth. Rather, all forms of meditation are fundamentally shaped by the way of life and dominant ideas found in each society. Although the basic capacities and tendencies of human beings have remained the same, the social and cultural forms of human life, including meditation practice, have varied. Thus, while we can see continuities in meditation practices from Gotama's teachings to today, the process, meaning, and purpose of meditation has substantially changed.

On the other hand, McMahan's description of the social and cultural context – the social imaginary – omits a crucial contextual factor. In what is otherwise an exceptionally rich and insightful account, McMahan does not explore the impact of perhaps the most important contextual factor affecting meditation: neoliberal capitalism. McMahan's analysis thus needs to be supplemented by an understanding of the ways in which neoliberal capitalism has shaped the rationale for and the practice of meditation.

Neoliberal capitalism and meditation practice

In simplest terms, capitalism is an economic system based on production for private profit rather than human needs, the control of economic resources by a small elite, and the exploitation of the majority of people within the production process. This system not only determines the ways in which goods and services are unevenly distributed to people along class lines, but also has a profound impact on all aspects of life, including how we see ourselves as human beings, the values we hold dear, how we relate to other human and non-human beings, and our connection with (or disconnection from) the natural world. The current neoliberal version of capitalism is exceptionally powerful in these respects as commodification and markets – facilitated by digital forms of communication, the internet, and social media – have colonized virtually all aspects of life,

Chapter 4: **The Role and Goal of Meditation**

including what were once considered the private spheres of the family and personal relationships. At the same time, the institutions of neoliberal capitalism disregard inclusivity, care, and the fulfillment of human needs, while intensifying ceaseless competition and conflict with others to gain power and wealth. These institutions valorize individual success, not the cooperative effort to build a society in which all human beings can flourish. Overall, the system facilitates and reinforces the cultivation of human tendencies toward greed and hatred while blocking the cultivation of human tendencies toward compassion and care.

In this way, neoliberal capitalism has a profound impact on meditation practice. At one level, meditation has become just another business opportunity, a way to profit from the increasing popularity of mindfulness meditation in therapeutic settings such as MBSR and mindfulness-based psychological interventions. In addition to the direct provision of mindfulness meditation services by entrepreneurs, there are a host of consultants who provide mindfulness programs to corporations and military institutions. Mindfulness meditation in these settings focuses on individual self-help and/or improvements in organizational efficiency, productivity, and profitability. This appropriation of mindfulness in a capitalist society led Ron Purser and others to characterize secular mindfulness as 'McMindfulness'. It negates the transformative potential of mindfulness and meditation, hijacking the practice to reinforce the individualistic focus of the profit-oriented society we live in.[77]

Yet, in emphasizing the negative aspects of commodified mindfulness, Purser has created an overly black-white dichotomy which misses some of the nuances and contradictory trends. It is true that corporations use mindfulness programs primarily to boost their bottom lines. Given the powerful impact of neoliberal capitalism, we shouldn't be surprised that, when a 2,500-year-old meditation technique meets up with a society in which capitalist economic and cultural values are hegemonic, it will be transformed fundamentally, and in not such good ways. On the other hand, as these mindfulness programs have grown more popular, hundreds of thousands of individuals have been introduced to meditation practice. For some of those people, their participation has not just lowered their stress and allowed them to function with more ease, but it has initiated a process of self-transformation and a new engagement with the world.

So while we can't simply characterize mindfulness meditation as a new tool of capitalist hegemony, we do need to recognize the ways in which capitalism warps meditation practice. And this occurs not just because meditation is sucked into the whirlwind of the profit generation machine. On an individual level, how we experience meditation and our objectives in doing this practice are profoundly shaped by a system which is based on an excessive focus on the needs and wants of individuals, rampant materialism and consumerism, and hierarchical structures which promote exploitation, oppression, and discrimination.

Neoliberal capitalism pushes individuals to see and experience meditation in a highly individualistic way; for many people it is all about how 'I' can benefit from meditation. We are also more likely to view the practice as a kind of consumer product with which to accumulate pleasant experiences in the meditative process, perhaps even to reach the ultimate goal of nirvana if we work hard enough. At the same time, given the pervasiveness of competition in a capitalist society, meditation practice can induce excessive pride and/ or punishing self-judgment as we compare ourselves to others in the race to become the 'best' meditator. In all these ways, capitalism profoundly shapes meditation practice and becomes a key contextual factor that we must recognize in understanding the process, meaning, and purpose of meditation today.

Problematic aspects of meditation retreats

In the context of contemporary western capitalist society, meditation is the primary (sometimes sole) practice of individuals who opt for the Buddhist spiritual path. The goal of meditation is to have a transformative experience in which one gains access to deep wisdom and insight about the world, facilitating a nirvanic experience. Many practitioners see meditation retreats as offering practitioners an ideal context or container for cultivating such a process. In

Chapter 4: **The Role and Goal of Meditation**

a retreat setting, we engage in the solitary experience of examining our sensations, emotions, and thoughts over an extended period of time. The goal is to overcome habitual conditioning and natural human tendencies in order to achieve what might be described as 'an embodied wisdom breakthrough' in which we have a direct connection with the way the way the world 'really is', and experience nirvana.

Let me offer a caveat. From my own experience, I have found that extended periods of meditation at a retreat can enrich my practice by strengthening my capacity to concentrate and be mindful. In a peaceful environment free from the distracting stimuli which fill much of our daily lives, we have the opportunity to pause and become more attuned to our habitual ways of thinking and feeling. The experience allows us to develop more capacity to respond creatively to life and its challenges. On meditation retreats, I have experienced moments of profound calm and important insights.

That said, given the role and goal of meditation within our society, meditation retreats are problematic in several respects. Because most meditation retreats focus almost entirely on individual meditation practice, two other dimensions of the Buddhist eightfold path – wisdom and ethics – are usually not cultivated to any significant extent. Yet, whether one is a secular Buddhist, a socially engaged Buddhist, or a follower of a traditional Buddhist lineage, a foundational idea in Buddhism is that progress on the spiritual path (however that goal is defined) requires the development of meditation, wisdom, and ethics as part of an integrated practice. The three are to be developed simultaneously, according to the capacity of each individual. They are all linked together and each feeds into the cultivation of the other two.

While ethics and wisdom aren't completely ignored in a meditation retreat, they're typically marginalized. For example, when a retreat begins, retreatants make a commitment to follow the five precepts, the basic ethical guidelines in Buddhism. During the rest of a retreat, though, this aspect of the dharmic path is rarely explored, unless a teacher offers a talk on some aspect of ethics. Just as the five precepts usually fade from view, so do two other key components of Buddhist ethics – appropriate speech and appropriate livelihood.

Since the retreatants are almost always in silence to limit distractions and to encourage the mindful awareness of their inner and external experiences, speech receives virtually no attention. The same goes for livelihood. How we earn a living, or perhaps engage in some form of unpaid work, constitutes one of the most important and impactful aspects of our lives. But this factor of the eightfold path almost never attracts sustained and careful examination.

In one respect, the retreat process does highlight the wisdom dimension of the eightfold path. The ultimate purpose of meditation is, after all, to gain wisdom or insight into our experiences and the world as we develop the capacity for mindfulness and concentrating the mind in meditation. However, while the embodied wisdom found in meditation is vitally important, other crucial ways of gaining wisdom are put aside in a traditional meditation retreat. We need to read, study, and reflect on topics related to the dharma if we want to develop a greater understanding of our existential condition and how to flourish as human beings. Virtually all lineages within Buddhism recognize the value of this method of gaining wisdom, but they neglect it in favor of the embodied wisdom achieved in meditation. Thus, in a meditation retreat, they discourage reading and study, which they presume interfere with developing a continuity of awareness attained through formal meditation sessions.

Further, we gain wisdom and insight in the context of social interaction, through dialogue and common activities with others. Sharing experiences, exchanging ideas, working together for a common end – all these modes of social interaction can have a profound impact on our ability to live a mindful and compassionate life. For example, we often gain a greater appreciation of the sense in which all human beings share a common experience of suffering and a common desire for happiness when we connect with other individuals in mindful dialogue. The current structure of meditation retreats forecloses this avenue for learning and wisdom.

In addition to overemphasizing individual meditation practice while marginalizing the other key dimensions of the eightfold path, ethics and wis-

Chapter 4: The Role and Goal of Meditation

dom, the other factor which makes retreats problematic is the notion that the ultimate goal of meditation is to achieve nirvana – a complete release from clinging and delusion. As I've noted, in a retreat setting, this notion can feed into either a desire to be superior to others or negative self-judgment and self-hatred, if we believe that we have not yet achieved that goal or are not capable of doing so. In short, meditation retreats can stoke the energies of the 'comparing mind', a mental state that Gotama warned about. The goal of achieving nirvana can become a kind of prize or special object that we long for to satisfy various needs, gaining something that no one else has, being special as a result. In this way, we can view the achievement of nirvana as a sign of our superiority.

Sitting in a meditation hall with other retreatants, I wonder if I am closer to nirvana than the meditator sitting next to me. Who is doing better? Who will be able to gain profound insights and be the special one? Who stands out? And then there's the downside if the goal of nirvana seems too far off or impossible to achieve. I may think: 'I'm not any good; I'll never be able to achieve enlightenment. What is wrong with me that I can't experience even a moment of complete release?' In this way, the pressure we experience in a capitalist society to compete with others and ourselves is reinforced, as is the tendency to cling to a particular outcome.

How might we avoid the problems inherent in meditation retreats while retaining their value in enriching practice? By integrating meditation practice with the ethical and social dimensions of Buddhism, as well as creating a sense of community among retreatants. By reconstructing the traditional retreat format to create a retreat structure which emphasizes social engagement, an exploration of ethics, and mindful dialogue.

If we want to deepen our commitment to and understanding of the dharmic path in all its facets, we need to develop a new type of intensive practice which encompasses and integrates them in its format and aims. This new form of intensive dharma practice needs to include significant periods of individual meditation, and would also have:

- ☆ Mindful dialogues in dyads and small groups about issues related to meditation, key Buddhist concepts, and how to live ethically.
- ☆ Group discussions on how to integrate key dharmic insights into our family and work lives, as well as in response to contemporary social and political problems.
- ☆ Opportunities for affinity groups (e.g., people of color) to meet to share experiences, exchange ideas, and support each other.
- ☆ Presentations and panels on various topics related to the dharma.

By offering these modes of group interaction, the sense of isolation and struggle that many people experience during retreats would diminish. In group settings, retreatants would have the opportunity to connect with and support each other as part of the process of developing greater wisdom, ethics, and compassion. To promote the development of community, specific attention should be given to retreatants' sangha experiences: how the sangha has supported their practice, what the aspirations of a sangha should be, and what problems they have encountered in sangha participation. The sharing of experiences and ideas would enliven the experience of sangha. Those who aren't in a sangha might learn about one in their area, or perhaps consider creating an online sangha with similarly situated retreatants. In short, a new form of intensive dharma practice which foregrounds ethics and sangha could offer an opportunity for dedicated practitioners to learn from each other and think more broadly about how to build stronger and more vital communities.

A different role and goal for meditation

From a secular, radically engaged perspective, I have argued that the most commonly prioritized version of meditation which has developed in the context of neoliberal capitalism is problematic in three respects. First, it is viewed as an individual pursuit, a practice performed by a solitary individual for their own benefit. Second, instead of being seen as one of three, complementary and interactive dimensions of the Buddhist path, along with wisdom and ethics,

Chapter 4: **The Role and Goal of Meditation**

it has become the primary process and context for practitioners. As a result, meditation and mindfulness practices no longer inform matters of ethics and social engagement. Finally, the ultimate goal of meditation for mainstream Buddhists is achieving access to an ultimate reality or absolute truth, and thus experiencing nirvana.

While recognizing the value of meditation for cultivating mindfulness and concentration, I believe that meditation is more fruitfully understood as a practice which, in conjunction with the cultivation of greater wisdom and ethics, enables us to develop essential insights and virtues for both individual flourishing in this life and contribute to creating a society in which everyone has the opportunity to flourish. Meditation doesn't lead to a vision of ultimate reality or complete freedom from all suffering. Instead, we need to view meditation as a grounded, socially embedded practice for people committed to a lifelong process of cultivating mindfulness, wisdom, and compassion.

Such an approach resonates with one of Gotama's own metaphors for dharma practice. As Stephen Batchelor has pointed out, Gotama compared the dharma practitioner to a skilled craftsperson; he 'likened the practitioner to a farmer irrigating a field, a fletcher fashioning an arrow, a carpenter shaping a piece of wood'.[78] Using the metaphor of dharma practice as a kind of skilled craft, we can understand how meditation might lead to both individual and social transformation in this life.

Like any novice craftsperson, when we first start to meditate, we have to acquire skills and knowledge if we want to make progress. The meditator needs to learn and practice various methods, understand the beneficial purposes the practice serves, and experience how various causes and conditions affect our meditation practice. We make progress with the help of the community we are part of, dharma teachers, the books and articles which we read, and the daily grind of practice, where we confront, again and again, the tenacious hold of the multifarious forms of our reactivity, and our tendency to hold on to our view of the self as a fixed, permanent entity.

To sustain and develop our practice, we need to cultivate the same attitudes and values a skilled craftsperson deploys – patience and perseverance – as we encounter the many frustrations of meditation practice, particularly in the beginning. We need a sense of openness and humility, a willingness to learn from those more experienced, at the same time recognizing that we'll encounter many causes and conditions over which we exercise little or no control as they affect our meditative experience. Finally, we understand how our meditation practice is beneficial, not just for ourselves, but for others, too.

Once we become more proficient at meditation, we usually experience beneficial results. We might call this the functional value of meditation. We have a greater capacity to relax; we become less stressed and more resilient in the face of life's challenges. But just as a skilled craftsperson can make objects which are not only functional but beautiful, so too can meditation go beyond stress reduction. Through meditation we can develop insight into the forces of reactivity and clinging, as well as the ways in which we are deeply connected to other beings in the ever-changing web of causes and conditions. And as we do this, we learn to shift the balance in our sensibility away from unskillful toward skillful modes of thinking and being in the world, to our own benefit and that of others.

We cultivate knowledge, skills, and virtues in meditation to promote our individual flourishing and progressive social change, but we're not trying to produce some perfect meditation result (or moment), free of all causes and conditions. However skilled at meditation we may become, we remain enmeshed in the natural world. There is no nirvana to reach, but in the process of shifting toward more skillful ways of being, we are fundamentally changed. This is a point that Winton Higgins has strongly emphasized. Citing Martha Nussbaum's notion of 'internal transcendence', Higgins quotes Nussbaum's remark that, 'what my argument urges us to reject as incoherent is the aspiration to leave behind altogether the constitutive conditions of our humanity, and to seek a life that is really the life of another sort of being – as if it were a higher and better life for us.'[79]

Chapter 4: **The Role and Goal of Meditation**

Essential virtues and insights

What are the particular virtues and insights which we need to cultivate in meditation? I'll discuss virtues and insights separately. The former involve ways of being, of relating to ourselves, others, and the world, as expressed in attitudes which have a strong affective component. The latter are ways of understanding and perceiving ourselves and the world. However, like the three components of the eightfold path (ethics, wisdom, and meditation), virtues and insights mutually interact and depend upon each other to develop.

Virtues

An essential list of virtues needs to begin with what Buddhists call the 'four immeasurables' (also known as the Brahmaviharas) of ancestral Buddhism, the quintessential heart qualities for someone on the Buddhist path, and an aspect of human flourishing:

- ☆ Loving kindness – a general, unconditional sense of friendliness toward ourselves and all other sentient beings.
- ☆ Compassion – an attitude of care and concern for ourselves and other beings in response to the difficult challenges that we face in life.
- ☆ Sympathetic joy – a positive feeling and sense of appreciation in relation to the happiness and good fortune of others.
- ☆ Equanimity – being balanced and unshaken in the midst of whatever we experience in life, be it good or bad.

We need to cultivate other virtues in meditation so as to flourish as human beings:

- ☆ Acceptance – not a sense of passivity and going along with whatever we experience, but rather an ability to be present and recognize whatever we experience, even when the experience is unpleasant or

not to our liking; acceptance must precede any wise response.
- ☆ Patience – the related ability to recognize and accept situations that are not what we want them to be at this moment, to allow time for causes and conditions (including our intentions and actions) to unfold.
- ☆ Perseverance and commitment – an attitude of 'stick-to-it-ness', of being on the path for the long haul, despite ups and downs.
- ☆ Non-judgmentalism – being less reflexively negative toward ourselves, another person, or an experience that does not please us or causes us to feel fearful, anxious, or out of control.
- ☆ Sense of wonder – an attitude of openness to the mystery and richness of life's experiences, a sense of its unknowability.

Insights

The key insights are linked to the virtues, and flow from Gotama's core teachings as well.

- ☆ The relationship between egocentrism and suffering – we increase our own suffering and that of others when we view ourselves as isolated and self-sufficient beings.
- ☆ Interdependence and mutual interaction – we are intrinsically connected and dependent upon other beings and the world at large.
- ☆ The complexity of life – the causes and conditions that frame our experiences are multiple and complex; very few mono-causal explanations provide helpful answers or complete explanations.
- ☆ Limited personal control – while we have some ability to effect changes and shape our lives, much of what we experience internally and externally is beyond our control.
- ☆ The pervasiveness of change – everything is in a state of flux (becoming rather than being), so change is inevitable; we invite suffering when we try to hold onto what we experience as pleasant or

Chapter 4: **The Role and Goal of Meditation**

push away what we experience as unpleasant.
- ☆ The limits of sense pleasure and external rewards – what is pleasant or appealing to us at the moment, based on a particular confluence of causes and conditions, will not endure as it is, and may in fact become unpleasant.
- ☆ Discernment, not judgment – we need to distinguish between the skillful ability to make important distinctions and evaluations on the one hand; and on the other, reflexively negative judgments based on our dislikes, fears, and anxieties.
- ☆ Beginner's mind – the sense of wonder and immediacy when we perceive experience less filtered through pre-existing habits of thought; when we face the complexity and mystery of life, we need to hold views less rigidly and be as open as we can to immediate experiences.

We can of course cultivate these virtues and insights outside of meditation practice, learning about them through reading and studying, thereby gaining a deeper and more sophisticated understanding of their role. At the same time, we can nurture these virtues and insights through our activities and relationships with others. Through participating in a community of practitioners and engaging in social action, we don't just improve the lives of others; we also cultivate and strengthen these virtues and insights in ourselves. In this sense, individual and collective transformation are inseparable.

Developing virtues and insights in meditation

In meditation, we cultivate the virtues and insights as we experience, in an embodied way and with increasing acuity and depth, the interplay of the contingent, complex, and unsatisfactory aspects of life. Meditation offers us an invaluable opportunity to witness, in a deliberate and compassionate way, our moment-to-moment experience – the pleasant and unpleasant – as a means of cultivating the virtues and insights crucial to human flourishing.

As anyone who meditates regularly knows, meditation is rarely a peak experience in Maslow's sense of a moment in which we have the highest happiness and fulfillment, suffused with a magnificent feeling of calm, peace, and insight.[80] Whatever particular meditation practice we're engaged in – sitting or walking, following the breath or noticing whatever arises, exploring the flow of experiences through choiceless awareness or concentrating the mind – meditation often involves periods of boredom or restlessness, as well as dealing with all sorts of difficult sensations, emotions, and thoughts. Yet, all these experiences help us to cultivate the virtues and insights we need to live more meaningfully.

Some forms of meditation directly support specific virtues and insights. For example, each of the 'immeasurables' inspires an associated concentration meditation practice which develops one of the virtues. By internally repeating certain phrases, we generate the ability to relate to ourselves and others with loving kindness, compassion, sympathetic joy, or equanimity.

Mindfulness meditation practices, which may include an anchor or primary object, such as noticing the movement of the breath in and out, can also help us to cultivate these virtues and insights. When (as often happens) we drift away from the anchor, carried away with a stream of sensations, emotions, or thoughts, we realize that we've done so and come back to the primary object of meditation. As Insight meditation teacher Sharon Salzberg has emphasized, this moment of recognition is actually the crux of mindfulness practice – 'the moment you realize you've been distracted is the magic moment... The act of beginning again is the essential art of meditation practice.'[81] At that moment, we remember to be mindful and stay in the present. However, the moment of recognition, to be really fruitful, needs to be more than just a bare awareness of 'whoops, drifted away'. It must also trigger a sense of compassion and loving kindness toward ourselves based on the recognition that we don't have some absolute control over our mental processes, and that drifting away is just a natural aspect of being human.

As we experience this process over and over again, other virtues are

Chapter 4: **The Role and Goal of Meditation**

cultivated: patience, acceptance, perseverance, and the ability to be less judgmental. The experience underscores important insights as well: the limits of our personal control, the causal relationship between egoic identification with our experiences and unnecessary suffering, and the ways in which our experiences arise from complex causes and conditions.

As we become more skillful in meditation practice, we become increasingly adept at noticing the ubiquity of change. Whatever we experience – a particular sensation, an emotion, or a thought – comes and goes; we have little control over the process. Really noticing the process of arising and passing away, developing the ability to experience this in a fully embodied way, is crucial for cultivating the key virtues and insights. This aspect of meditation practice helps us to gain deeper wisdom, particularly of impermanence. We experience on a granular level our basic situation as human beings; we want our life to be pleasant and rewarding, but we can't hold on to that which we like and desire. We can't grasp onto the objects of our experience: they will be there one moment and gone the next. Conversely, when we fully realize the ubiquity of change, we understand that we only cause ourselves and others more suffering when we harden ourselves to or push away from what we consider to be unpleasant and painful, whether it's a painful knee or a troubling thought that just won't go away. Just as we can't hold onto the pleasant, the unpleasant and painful will also pass away as the causes and conditions supporting them break up.

Some forms of meditation practice, such as choiceless awareness and Soto Zen *shikintaza* or 'just sitting', also help us to cultivate essential virtues and insights but they are not based on using an anchor or primary object. The crux of meditation for Zen teacher Barry Magid is 'simply being present and responsive to each moment as it is, including an awareness of our thoughts and emotional resistances as just momentary phenomena that we experience as they pass.'[82] This form of meditation emphasizes an open receptivity to whatever experience comes up. But like mindfulness meditation based on an anchor, the ability to be present in the midst of all the aspects of life – pleasant and unpleasant – depends on developing the whole array of virtues and insights, from an understanding of the causes of suffering to becoming more patient and accepting, to recognizing the complex web of causes and conditions of which we are just one part.

Finally, meditation initiates us into the mystery and unknowability of life, what Batchelor calls the everyday sublime. Despite our growing knowledge in the physical and social sciences, allowing us to create ever more advanced forms of technology and culture, we have only a partial understanding of ourselves and the world. The web of causes and conditions in flux is too complex for us to grasp.

When we discern our limits in this regard, we understand the world exceeds our capacity to represent it in words. Everything we encounter in everyday life – a stream, a sunset, a street corner, and so on – has a richness beyond our capacity to explain it. This sublimity of everyday experience 'brings the calculating mind to a stop, leaving one speechless, overwhelmed with wonder or terror.'[83] The everyday sublime thus involves a sense of awe, a need to doubt and question, and a basic humility.

Some meditation practices focus on cultivating this sense of wonder and the value of the 'beginner's mind' which is open to the mystery of life – a vital part of human flourishing. In the Korean Sŏn school the centrality of doubt and the injunction to be open to experience is encapsulated in the practice question 'What is this?'. In a series of dharma talks on this form of meditation, Martine Batchelor and Stephen Batchelor show how this question doesn't seek to uncover the nature of reality but rather instills a profound sense of doubt and openness.[84]

A transformative process

Through meditation, we can develop deep insight into the forces of reactivity and clinging, as well as the ways in which we are embedded with other beings in the ever-changing flow of causes and conditions. We can also begin to appreciate the ways in which our world is mysterious and unknowable, to encounter the everyday sublime. In this process, we are increasingly able to move from unskillful to skillful modes of thinking and being in the world; and with this shift, to promote the flourishing of ourselves and all other beings.

This is truly a transformative process, but it does not lead to any breakthrough moment in which we are free, either temporarily or permanently, of all causes and conditions. However skilled at meditation we become, we remain firmly embedded in the natural world. There is no nirvana to reach in meditation in the traditional sense, but in the process of shifting toward more skillful ways of being, we can fundamentally change ourselves and contribute to social transformation. By cultivating these key virtues and insights, we create the basis for living a calmer, happier, and more fulfilling life in this world, whatever the causes and conditions that we experience. Our purpose in meditation is thus to cultivate these virtues and insights to the extent that we can. They are essential to a life of genuine happiness and fulfillment, one in which we and others can lead meaningful and ethical lives.

Chapter 5
Not-self and the Bodhisattva Path

In addition to the Four Noble Truths and the eightfold path, two of the most important Buddhist concepts are the notion of not-self (anattā) and the bodhisattava path as the model for an enlightened human being. For Buddhists, the idea of not-self represents a radical rejection of the common view we have of ourselves as an 'I' or 'me' who is a separate, substantial entity. The reality that the self is a process is one of the so-called three basic characteristics or marks of existence in Buddhism that I have previously discussed: impermanence (*anicca*), suffering (dukkha), and not-self. Mainstream Buddhists believe that these core experiences mold the way we perceive ourselves and the world, so we need to gain deep insight into them.

The other key notion, particularly in Mahayana Buddhism, is that of the bodhisattva, which provides an inspiration and model for the social and ethical dimensions of the Buddhist path. When contemporary Buddhists reach for a uniquely Buddhist response to the social problems that we face today, they often invoke the bodhisattva as the exemplar for an activist. Not-self and the bodhisattva path thus represent respectively distinctive Buddhist understandings of the path to individual transformation and to the socio-ethical responsibilities of human beings.

In this chapter, I rethink not-self and the bodhisattva path from a secular, radically engaged perspective. I seek to reveal their limitations as presented in mainstream Buddhist discourse, while offering an alternative way of understanding the kernel of truth that each reveals. To do so, we need to situate them within a naturalistic and socio-historical frame while relating each notion to the goal of human flourishing for all.

The three marks of existence: as insights for reducing suffering

Before we delve into not-self in some detail, we need to discern how conventional Buddhist doctrine understands the three marks of existence. It tends to treat them not as direct and accessible experiences but as truths about the way things are. In Chapter 2 I discussed Stephen Batchelor's valuable critique of the conventional treatment of the three marks as truth claims about the way things are in the context of the Four Noble Truths. This change happened with the emergence of Buddhism as an institutionalized religion after Gotama's death, transforming Gotama's pragmatic and ethical insights into fixed beliefs about an ultimate reality. Philosophers call this 'ontologization'.

The same distortion has overtaken the three marks of existence, rendering them as three basic truths about objective reality. They supposedly describe the way the world really is behind the mask of forms and appearances. For ancestral Buddhists, these three marks constitute one component of a 'right view' of the world, the first of the eight 'folds' of the path.

In my view, we could understand the three marks more fruitfully as three pervasive factors of human experience which can come to mold our existential-psychological experience of the world. They arise in our experience through the mutual interaction of our uniquely human capacities and tendencies, social conditions, and natural processes. When we understand the three marks in this way, we'll understand their salience in shaping our lived experience, rather than as universal characteristics of reality.

We can rethink impermanence (anicca) – another core concept in Buddhism – in similar terms. Gotama emphasized that we suffer more than we need to because we don't deeply understand that everything is impermanent. We have a tendency to want to hold on to the things and processes that are pleasant to us. But the conditions of our existence are changing all the time; we simply

Chapter 5: **Not-self and the Bodhisattva Path**

cannot hold on to or fix in place what we experience as pleasant. Conversely, that which is unpleasant and which we want to push away will not remain forever; all phenomena, being impermanent, will cease to exist.

The combined impact of our failure to grasp the ubiquity of impermanence and our tendency to crave (to want to hold on to the pleasant and push away the unpleasant) creates unnecessary suffering. We don't need to elevate impermanence to the realm of Truth to understand how it impacts on our lived experience.

While reading about and reflecting on the nature of impermanence helps us, meditative practice turns it into a visceral rather than merely cognitive wisdom that deflects our clinging and grasping tendencies. In meditation we can observe how things and processes are changing all the time. The pain in the back that seems constant is actually a shifting array of sensations and feelings. A troubling thought emerges and then disappears. The pleasant sensation of a cool breeze turns into a chill wind. When we can relax into our experiences with the understanding that change is ever-present, we are less likely to suffer.

This example offers a valuable insight into how impermanence affects our experience of suffering. Yet we can't jump from this insight to the conclusion that impermanence is a fundamental characteristic of existence. Why is impermanence any more fundamental or basic as an ontological attribute than permanence? One could say the fact that things change all the time is itself a permanent aspect of existence. Our tendency to crave also seems permanent, as is our need to breathe to stay alive. Permanence is thus just as significant a factor in our experience as is impermanence. We cannot even recognize impermanence unless we have the backdrop of something permanent with which to notice impermanence. The Greek philosopher Heraclitus highlighted the constant change or flux of existence when he said that 'No man steps in the same river twice,' but we experience the river as flowing (i.e., changing) because there are relatively permanent riverbanks between which the river flows. Similarly, we perceive the clouds that move across the sky (an image often used by Buddhist teachers to represent the evanescent nature of thoughts) as temporary phenomena because they move through what appears to us as a permanent sky.

Likewise, the Buddhist concept of not-self captures an important factor in our experience but does not represent an ontological truth. Gotama rightfully asserted that if we try to find the self – defined as a substantial, independent entity which has complete control over its experience – it is nowhere to be found. When we look for such a self, what we find instead are phenomena in discrete areas of experience; namely, in the body, feeling-tones, perceptions, moods and emotions, and cognition. But because we tend to believe that we have a substantial self beyond these discrete experiences, we tend to over-identify with experiential phenomena. This process of over-identification, combined with the human tendency to crave, causes unnecessary suffering. We view as 'I', 'me' and 'mine' phenomena which we don't control, phenomena that arise from myriad impersonal and interconnected causes. This 'selfing' – feeding the illusion of a separate, substantial self – leads to the intensification and narrative elaboration of the pleasant or unpleasant experiences which we have.

Gotama refused to buy into a dichotomy between an ontologically false view of the self and the ontologically correct view of not-self. As I noted in Chapter 2, the purpose of Gotama's teachings on anatta was to offer us a strategy for how to weaken the self-conception of a separate self so we could suffer less. As Thanissaro Bhikkhu has argued, Gotama was trying to show us 'how to use perceptions of self and not-self as strategies leading to a happiness that's reliable and true.' What he was *not* offering was a particular doctrine of *what the self is or isn't* in some ontological sense.[85]

Finally, we should see suffering as an integral part of the human condition rather than as a basic attribute of reality. Gotama taught that suffering is woven into every human life, from the mildest discomfort or stress, through our inevitable vulnerability and mortality, to the most excruciating anguish or misery. And his primary goal as a teacher was to minimize suffering: 'Both formerly & now, it is only stress that I describe, and the cessation of stress.'[86]

Gotama offered meditative practices and a way of life which help us to reduce suffering. Yet we have happiness and joy in our life, too, as he noted.

So, why is dukkha, rather than happiness, a primary characteristic or mark of existence? There seems to be no compelling reason to elevate dukkha to a more basic ontological status than happiness.

As with his teachings on impermanence and not-self, we can see Gotama's teachings on suffering as a therapeutic strategy rather than as an assertion of a truth claim. He highlights the pervasiveness of suffering in our lives; and then proposes a radical shift in our way of life to attain happiness. As Gotama noted, some suffering is completely inevitable; human beings cannot avoid illness, aging, the loss of those we love, disappointment and death, but we add an extra layer to our suffering by reacting badly to the difficulties we encounter. We can certainly lessen this kind of suffering, which arises from the way we relate to the ubiquity of change in our lives and how we view ourselves. When we have a false understanding of ourselves and don't recognize the ubiquity of change, we suffer more than we have to

Rethinking not-self, critiquing Garfield

Of the three fundamental marks or characteristics of existence, not-self is the most complex and controversial. That we suffer in various ways and that we constantly experience change is obvious; they make intuitive sense. Not-self is less clear and not as obvious. The meaning and role of this concept has stirred up vigorous debate among Buddhists. It also presents more of an existential and psychological challenge to practitioners. How do we move from a delusional notion of self to a direct experience of not-self? Does the loss of one's sense of self mean a complete loss of control? Can one function in the world from a stance of not-self?

For some practitioners, these difficult questions can create anxiety and dread. Buddhist teachers assert that gaining experiential insight into not-self, along with the other two marks, is a necessary condition for making progress on the spiritual path. The experience of not-self may leave some practitioners in a state of anxiety, while failure to have it might look like a defeat. This problem arises precisely because not-self has been framed as an ontological issue.

For traditional Buddhists, having a correct view of the self and gaining experiential insight into this truth enables one to achieve the ultimate goal of spiritual practice – nirvana, the complete cessation of suffering. For contemporary Buddhists who subscribe to what David McMahan terms Buddhist modernism,[87] nirvana as a transcendent state in which one is completely free of suffering forever may not be accessible or even desirable. Yet, like traditional Buddhists, Buddhist modernists believe that the attempt to move toward a more mindful and compassionate mode of being in this life crucially depends on shifting from our default, delusory sense of self to understanding and experiencing ourselves as contingent not-selves to the extent that we can.

Traditional and modernist Buddhists see the delusory sense of self as the source of craving, and thus of suffering in all its many dimensions. For them it constitutes a universal problem insofar as all human beings have a natural tendency to fall for this cognitive illusion and work from a false view of the self and thus become their own worst enemies in magnifying their suffering.

In what follows I offer a different perspective on not-self, one that shifts the discussion from an epistemological and ontological issue to an ethically informed exploration of the existential, psychological, and social causes of various forms of selfing. I present this perspective by engaging with the arguments offered by Jay Garfield in his book, *Losing Ourselves: Learning to Live Without a Self*. Garfield subscribes to the view that the self, as commonly understood, is a fundamental cognitive illusion which obscures the ontological truth of not-self. He draws on both Western and Buddhist philosophers to support this position. While his arguments are based in large part on the writings of Mahayana Buddhists such as Chandrakirti and Shantideva, as well as the Tibetan Buddhist Tsongkhapa, he puts aside ancestral Buddhist notions like rebirth, karma and nirvana. He argues that Buddhist philosophical perspectives on the self, as well as those of philosophers like Hume and Heidegger, provide us with a correct understanding of ourselves and the world.[88]

What does Garfield mean by the self? His reference points are the ancient Indian concept of ātman, which Gotama rejected, and the notion of the soul in

Chapter 5: **Not-self and the Bodhisattva Path**

Christian theology. While quite different in some respects, the Vedic atman and the Christian soul share the following assumptions about the self:

- ☆ The self exists *prior to and independent of* the world we experience.
- ☆ The self constitutes a *unity* which enjoys a unified experience of itself in the world.
- ☆ The self presupposes a duality between a subject (i.e., the self) and the objects of its experience. In this *subject-object duality* we experience ourselves as subjects and everything else as objects.
- ☆ We exercise free will, or unconstrained *agency*.

Taken together, these conceptual ingredients constitute 'the illusion that we stand outside of and against the world. We take ourselves pre-reflectively to be singularities: not participants in the world, but spectators of the world, and agents of actions directed on that world.'[89]

This notion of self falsifies who and how we are as human beings – it is ontologically false – Garfield argues. We should instead see ourselves as *persons*, as organisms who are embedded and embodied in the world; we are the products of the web of causes and conditions (including our own actions) that constitute us at any given moment. As he puts it, while 'the self is taken to be preexistent, primordial, unitary, and transcendent of the world of objects … the person is constructed; the person is dependent on the psychophysical and social network in which it is realized'.[90]

Garfield explains how our very sense of ourselves as distinct individuals develops in a social context – initially, in the relationship between the infant and their primary caregivers. That is, we come to see ourselves as separate beings only through our awareness of, and our recognition by, 'second persons'. There is no primordial 'I' that exists prior to or as a foundation of this social interaction.

How we develop as persons is a complex product of our biologically evolved structure and capacities, the psychological context, and social and cultural norms. These dimensions of our existence mutually interact with each other. Our psychological characteristics and social structures are limited by our biological structures and capacities, yet the psychological and social dimensions constrain and affect our biological development as well. Garfield thus rejects a reductionist perspective in which we are ultimately the product of physical and biological forces.

Is the notion of a separate, substantial self a 'hardwired' cognitive illusion?

Garfield offers a valid critique of a particular notion of the self which depicts us as isolated, separate beings, and correctly emphasizes the ways in which we're essentially social beings. But there's a problem with his account. Garfield asserts that we're naturally inclined to adopt the illusion of an isolated self and all that it entails. While his argument doesn't depend on transcendence through attainment of nirvana, he closely follows the traditional Buddhist view that the notion of the self is a universal characteristic of human beings, as is the tendency to crave. For him we suffer because, as human beings, we naturally crave and have a false sense of the self.

To the extent that our biology and survival instinct predispose us to self-ing, the Buddhist view that suffering results from craving (for secular Buddhists, read reactivity in general) remains a valid insight. As biological organisms, we do tend to identify most strongly with our own experiences, to prefer our own perspective, and to be most concerned with our own situation. Given the ubiquity of change and our relative lack of control over the events in our life, this results in our experiencing suffering above and beyond the direct physical and emotional pains that occur as an inevitable part of life.

Yet (and this is the key point), it's a mistake to view selfing as a dichotomous phenomenon, as Garfield does. From his perspective, either one does not engage in selfing because one recognizes the reality that we are persons (i.e., we have achieved a state of not-self) or one is fully engaged in selfing based on a delusory notion of the separate self. In my view, it is more fruitful to see selfing as an aspect of human experience which spans a continuum. Based on

Chapter 5: **Not-self and the Bodhisattva Path**

the mutual interaction of biological, psychological, and social factors, different forms of selfing exist. This continuum ranges from forms of selfing in which we see ourselves as absolutely separate and independent subjects, as in notions of the soul or atman, to looser, more flexible forms of selfing.

Thus, rather than a universal characteristic of human beings, the notion of an atman/soul/self is *only one* of the ways in which our sense and notion of self is shaped by biological, psychological, and social factors. The key question is why and how this particular notion of self arises. Why is it that so many of us come to see ourselves as, among other things, isolated beings, as subjects who are separate from and opposed to objects in the world?

Different societies, different notions of the self

Garfield's analysis of the development of persons provides us with a way of addressing these questions. As he points out, we become persons in a complex process in which biological structures and tendencies, psychological processes, and social forces mutually interact. It follows that particular combinations of these factors will mold our conceptions of how we see ourselves, of how we experience ourselves as human beings. This means that instead of just one, false notion of the self that is based on a cognitive illusion, there are a range of views of the self. A voluminous literature addresses this topic, primarily located in the field of cultural psychology. It contrasts cultures which have an individualistic notion of the self with those that foster a more collective identity.[91]

Although the notion of a separate, isolated self emerged in ancient cultures, including in the ideas of the atman and the soul, radical theorists have emphasized for quite some time that a particular version of this notion became more widespread with the emergence of capitalism. The reification of a person into a separate self, which Garfield sees as the product of a universal cognitive illusion, is actually historically contingent, these theorists suggest. In the modern era this notion reflects the development of a society and economy which reifies human beings themselves. In a capitalist society, the social connections between human beings are obscured and we come to see ourselves as isolated beings competing for resources and power in the market. The social structures and processes which produce this conception receive philosophical elaboration in the form of theories of individualism which are consistent with and justify the system.

This philosophical elaboration occurred very early on in the development of capitalism. C.B. Macpherson, the Canadian political philosopher, analyzed how a theory of possessive individualism underlay the writings of Hobbes, Locke, and other 17th century philosophers. One of the key assumptions of this perspective is that 'the individual is essentially the proprietor of his own person and capacities.'[92] This notion of the self closely resembles the view of the self as a separate, isolated being which Garfield critiques.

The false dualism of self and not-self

The dualism which Garfield posits between the self and the person is similar in form to the self/not-self dichotomy in ancestral Buddhism; and shares the same basic problem. By positing a dichotomy between a false notion of the self and a true notion of a person (not-self), Garfield transforms the Buddha's pragmatic and ethical insights about how a certain notion of the self leads to suffering into an epistemological and ontological issue, just as traditional Buddhists have done with the self/not-self dichotomy.

In his writings, Stephen Batchelor has consistently rejected the dualistic approach to self and not-self, arguing that ontologizing these notions obscures Gotama's primary purpose. Batchelor explained:

> Gotama is interested in what people can *do*, not with what they *are*. The task he proposes entails distinguishing between what is to be accepted as the natural condition of life itself (the unfolding of experience) and what is to be let go of (reactivity). ... The liberating insight he proposes is *not* the realization that there is no self but the realization that I am not the same as or reducible to any or all of the five bundles [of experience] that constitute me...[93]

Chapter 5: **Not-self and the Bodhisattva Path**

As I noted above, Thanissaro Bhikkhu has argued that Gotama's teachings on not-self offer us a strategy for how to move away from a view of self that causes suffering. To reduce suffering, Gotama is 'not trying to deprive us of our strategies for happiness; he's actually trying to show us how to expand and refine them so that we can find a happiness better than any happiness we've ever known.'[94] Of course, as a traditional Theravada Buddhist, Thanissaro Bhikkhu sees the Buddha's pedagogical strategies as providing us the resources to let go of our attachments. From a secular, radically engaged perspective, we should instead see these as strategies that enable us to flourish more in this world.

Thus, it is more fruitful to view the issue of not-self through a pragmatic and ethical lens than as an ontological issue. Our challenge here is twofold. First, to understand how the mutual interaction of biological, psychological, and social factors leads to a variety of ways in which we see who we are, including as separate, self-interested beings. And second, to identify the skills and virtues needed to move us away from egocentricity toward a more open, compassionate, and relational mode of being. Loosening the grip of the egotistical self is vital for both individual and social transformation. In this endeavor we need an approach which eschews dualisms, and instead explores the specific causes and conditions which influence how we view and relate to ourselves, others, and the world.

Rethinking the bodhisattva path

For traditional and modernistic Buddhists, not-self is a radical concept which challenges us to transform ourselves as individuals on the path to liberation. The bodhisattva path represents for many Buddhists an equally radical challenge to how we live our lives. Instead of just aiming to achieve his or her own complete liberation from suffering the bodhisattva works ceaselessly to achieve the complete liberation of all beings. In fact, until all of them have attained nirvana, the bodhisattva – who is fully capable of achieving nirvana – refuses the leap into such a state of complete freedom and happiness. In this sense, he or she is the ultimate embodiment of a life which expresses the core Buddhist values of universal compassion and love. For many Buddhists, the aspiration to become a bodhisattava crystallizes Buddhist values and insights, transforming their interpersonal lives and their social engagement with the problems that we all face.

Although the bodhisattva ideal arose in the Mahayana tradition, modern-day Buddhist teachers in Insight and other Theravada lineages also teach it as an ideal way of being in the world. Socially-engaged Buddhists exemplify this trend; the bodhisattva models the way forward for someone who works ceaselessly and unselfishly to remedy the suffering experienced by humans and other beings. David Loy, a Zen Buddhist at the forefront of integrating Buddhism with social activism, argues that the bodhisattva provides us with essential resources to respond wisely to the climatic and ecological crisis that we face today. Loy calls for us to take up the work of being 'ecosattvas', committed to saving the world from ecological disaster and thus stopping the suffering this crisis inflicts on all beings.[95]

I recognize the power of the bodhisattva model and the positive effect it has had on many people. But I have always balked at the invocation of the bodhisattva as the ideal way of treading the path. Many Buddhists gain inspiration from the first of the four bodhisattva vows: 'The many beings are numberless; I vow to save them.' Yet I find it somewhat hyperbolic and hollow. In the first place, the bodhisattva path presupposes the notion of nirvana as an ultimate realm of complete freedom from suffering, which as a secular Buddhist I reject. At the same time, as a radically engaged Buddhist, I find the model of the bodhisattva as some heroic individual inconsistent with the kind of mass democratic movement for social change that we need. If we are seeking to promote individual flourishing and a society in which all people have the opportunity to flourish, we will need a different kind of model of social engagement.

The essential task: reduce suffering and promote flourishing

Although the bodhisattva path is often discussed in terms of how we can live skillfully and compassionately in the world, this path is still integrally connected to the view that complete freedom from suffering can be obtained. The bodhisattva's ultimate goal, after all, is to help all beings attain nirvana and the complete

Chapter 5: **Not-self and the Bodhisattva Path**

release from suffering. As a secular Buddhist, it seems to me that the goal of realizing such a state, or even aspiring to achieve such a state with the knowledge that one is unlikely to attain it, takes us away from what I see as the goal of the path – human flourishing and the well-being of other sentient beings in this life.

My discomfort with this aspect of the bodhisattva model was clarified when I reread Albert Camus's *The Plague*, a novel about a bacterial plague that suddenly strikes Oran, a town in Algeria, and how individuals in the town respond to the crisis.[96] Written during the second world war, the book has a deeply ethical dimension. In a discussion of existentialism and Buddhist ethics, Winton Higgins notes that Camus's novel is in part an allegory about the evil and suffering caused by Nazism, and the divergent ways in which people respond.[97] A passage about a third of the way into the book offers a vivid contrast between two approaches: the traditional, religious goal of overcoming suffering by achieving ultimate happiness and freedom outside the conditioned, interconnected world in which we live, and the secular goal of reducing suffering and promoting human flourishing in this world. For me, this contrast provides an apt illustration of my first concern about the bodhisattva path.

The protagonist and narrator of the book is a physician, Dr. Bernard Rieux. Throughout the plague, he works tirelessly to ease the suffering of his patients. Other characters in the book also engage in these efforts in their own way, including a Catholic priest, Father Paneloux. The priest views this crisis through the lens of an orthodox religious believer; his efforts to help the sick are part of his mission to save human souls even in the midst of an inexplicably terrible event. At the height of the plague's destructive phase, Rieux and Paneloux – both exhausted by their unceasing efforts – discuss the horror of seeing children suffer and die from the plague:

> 'I understand,' Paneloux said in a low voice. 'That sort of thing is revolting because it passes our human understanding. But perhaps we should love what we cannot understand.'
> Rieux straightened up slowly. He glanced at Paneloux, summoning

to his gaze all his strength and fervour he could muster against his weariness. Then he shook his head.

'No, Father. I've a very different idea of love. And until my dying day I shall refuse to love a scheme of things in which children are put to torture.'

A shade of disquietude crossed the priest's face. He was silent for a moment. Then, 'Ah doctor,' he said sadly, 'I've just realized what is meant by "grace".'

Rieux had sunk back again on his bench. His lassitude had returned and from its depths he spoke more gently.

'It's something I haven't got; that I know. But I'd rather not discuss that with you. We're working for something side by side that unites us – beyond blasphemy and prayers. And it's the only thing that matters.'

Paneloux sat down beside Rieux. It was obvious that he was deeply moved.

'Yes, yes,' he said, 'you, too, are working for man's salvation.' Rieux tried to smile.

'Salvation's much too big a word for me. I don't aim so high. I'm concerned with man's health; and for me his health comes first.'[98]

Rieux's goal, his vocation, is about bettering the condition of human beings in this life; it's not about finding salvation in another realm or explaining the horrible suffering that humans experience in the context of possible salvation. His response to Paneloux seems to me to capture the essential difference between a secular Buddhist ethics and a traditional, religious approach in terms of their ultimate goals. For Rieux, it is working with others to reduce suffering and promote human flourishing in this life; for Paneloux, it is 'saving souls'.

While there isn't an exact analogy between Paneloux's Catholicism and traditional Buddhism, the ultimate goals of Paneloux and a bodhisattva are

Chapter 5: **Not-self and the Bodhisattva Path**

similar: to end suffering completely by guiding individuals to a realm in which all suffering has disappeared. If we replace the term salvation with enlightenment or nirvana, the goal of traditional forms of Buddhism, we can apply Rieux's response to the Buddhist who embraces the bodhisattva's vow to help all sentient beings reach nirvana. To a traditional Buddhist interlocutor, Rieux would say: 'Enlightenment's much too big a word for me. I don't aim so high. I'm concerned with human flourishing; and for me flourishing comes first.'

Solidarity, not heroism

The bodhisattva represents a problematic kind of heroic model of spiritual attainment. Despite the unfathomable enormity of the task, the bodhisattva commits to do whatever it takes to save all beings, irrespective of the obstacles. This superhuman effort is similar to the heroic legend of Gotama's enlightenment. According to the early texts, Gotama went through all sorts of ordeals to attain liberation. At one point, he was close to death from practicing an extreme form of asceticism. After rejecting this approach, he engaged in a different approach but one that was nonetheless equally arduous; he decided to sit under a peepul tree, the *ficus religiosa*, and meditate for however long it took to gain full realization. And, of course, as these same texts tell us, he ultimately prevailed, even in the face of the Evil One Mara's strategies to defeat him.

While I understand the appeal of this heroic struggle, it offers an inappropriate model for both spiritual transformation and political engagement. As a secular, radically engaged Buddhist, I don't believe that we need to find heroes who can lead us to a promised land. Rather, our challenge is to develop a movement in which thousands of committed, mindful and compassionate activists work together to address the environmental and social crises we face. In short, our model for spiritual transformation and social engagement should be the solidarity of activists co-creating a new world.

The model of the hero is deeply gendered. The heroic striver for spiritual attainment or leader of movements is typically associated with qualities and virtues purportedly associated with masculinity, such as strength, vigor, courage, and rationality. Women, who putatively lack these qualities, are consigned to secondary, supportive roles. The patriarchy and misogyny found within traditional Buddhism and other spiritual traditions, as well as in political movements, reflects the subordination and marginalization of women.

Interestingly, contemporary Buddhists exhibit a growing recognition of the limitations of the heroic model, and of the need to envisage an alternative path of spiritual attainment, one more grounded in connections and relationships. Thus, Janet Surrey and Samuel Shem's fictional biography of the life of Yasodharā in *The Buddha's Wife* attempts to offer 'the symbolic possibility of a complementary path that leads to a doorway of profound spiritual maturation and the awakening of wisdom and compassion, often through living deeply with others – beyond the solitary heroic journey'.[99]

In addition, the historical record reveals the potential problem of emphasizing the role of heroes in the context of spiritual traditions and politics. The tendency of religions and political organizations to become dominated by a charismatic leader has often resulted in the degeneration of these movements into top-down, hierarchical, and dogmatic institutions. We've all heard how some spiritual movements have become cults in which gurus gain absolute power and engage in harmful actions toward their followers, including sexual assault. In the political realm, the extreme version of this process manifests when a radical movement is dominated by a dictator, a Stalin or a Mao, who becomes the embodiment of revolution, the Great Leader and Hero of the People.

Of course, there have been great, charismatic leaders such as Gandhi, Dr. Martin Luther King, Jr., BR Ambedkar and Nelson Mandela, who are revered by Buddhists and among political activists as exemplars of peace, courage, compassion, and a deep commitment to social change. And rightly so. But while they inspire us and have had an important and positive impact, they should not be the primary models for our spiritual transformation or political activism.

While charismatic leaders can play a key role, the success of any movement which has helped to expand human rights and create a more just society, depends on the thousands of people who work behind the scenes as activists

Chapter 5: **Not-self and the Bodhisattva Path**

and organizers. Mostly unrecognized, they do the vital work of recruiting and developing others to join the movement and take action for social change. Using their organizational, educational, and communication skills, they build and sustain the organizations and movements which challenge exploitative and oppressive social systems. Without this broad layer of activists, no organization or movement can achieve its goals. In this context, two important examples are Ella Baker and Robert Moses, who played crucial roles in the US civil rights movement by mentoring individuals and fostering their leadership skills. Through their words and actions, they promoted a democratic movement to challenge racism and poverty in the USA. And for every Baker or Moses, dozens of others proved themselves equally essential in building a strong civil rights movement.

Co-creating change through solidarity and democracy
Very few of us can be charismatic leaders, heroes of spiritual attainment or the great leaders of political movements. But each of us can contribute in our own ways to help build a society which promotes the flourishing of all human beings. And it is precisely by working together, in solidarity with others, melding our strengths and weaknesses, that we can develop successful political movements. If we're to contribute effectively to creating a better world, we need to shift our aspirations and orientation from an individualistic, leader-centric model of spiritual attainment and political change to a process in which we co-create individual and social transformation. Our path is not predetermined and the end is not set in advance. Together, we figure out the direction in which to head, the strategies and tactics we need, and our ultimate goals.

This shift in turn highlights the priority of building democratic communities and organizations in which we can co-create change: unions, non-profit organizations, political groups, and movement coalitions. For Buddhist practitioners it means forging democratic and inclusive communities. As the third of the three jewels of Buddhism, the role of spiritual communities has grown in salience in recent years.

One of the strongest proponents of this view was Thich Nhat Hanh, a well-known teacher and a founding figure of socially engaged Buddhism. In contrast to those who foreground meditation as the crux of Buddhist practice, Thich Nhat Hanh emphasized the vital role played by community on the path to individual and social transformation. In closing remarks to over two thousand people attending his Day of Mindfulness at Spirit Rock Center in Woodacre, California in October 1993, he said:

> It is possible the next Buddha will not take the form of an individual. The next Buddha may take the form of a community, a community practicing understanding and loving kindness, a community practicing mindful living. And the practice can be carried out as a group, as a city, as a nation.[100]

For sanghas and political groups to have a transformative impact, they need to be democratically run, based on mutual respect between participants. Sanghas and activist organizations must promote the equal participation of members, each sharing the strengths and resources that they bring to the group, however unevenly distributed those resources might be. The values and practices we are trying to create in a society must be modelled in our communities and organisations. When we relate to each other in a spirit of equality, respect, and care, as comrades and spiritual friends, we develop and reinforce the qualities and virtues which meditation and other individual practices also promote. We reinforce a deeper sense of our common humanity, the ability to override egocentric tendencies, a clearer understanding of ourselves and the world, and a greater capacity for compassion and love.

We can certainly take inspiration from Gotama, the bodhisattvas, and the great political and religious leaders, but our path, our aspirations, must take root in our ongoing efforts to co-create the transformative changes that we seek, and to epitomize them in our own communities.

Chapter 6
Rethinking Left Politics

Let me begin with a disclaimer. In this chapter I'm not attempting to offer a comprehensive perspective on the theory and practice of Left politics. In the face of many setbacks to their efforts to radically transform the capitalist system, Leftists of all stripes have always engaged in a process of assessment, evaluation, internal criticism, and revision. They have done so on many different levels: debates over basic philosophical concepts and theories of history; controversies over political economy; arguments regarding the appropriate strategies and tactics that will lead to fundamental change; and disputes over the structures and processes of Left organizations. My aim in this chapter is more modest: to set out the ways in which core Buddhist ideas and practices can help radical movements and groups drive social change. How can a secular, radically engaged version of Buddhism help sustain activism and a healthy internal life in Left movements?

By the term 'Left', I'm referring to the broad array of political groups and trends which seek either to reform the current systems of exploitation and oppression or to develop radical movements whose objective is to replace such systems with new, creative ones. So, the Left in this sense includes anarchists, social democrats, radical socialists, and communists. It also includes movements whose focus is not the reform or abolition of capitalism per se, but challenging and upending other systems of oppression, such as racism, sexism, and homophobia.

I locate myself in the broader Left as a democratic socialist, a member of the Democratic Socialists of America (DSA), a group in the USA. In recent years its membership has increased and it has gained a more significant (if still limited) influence. In my twenties and thirties, I embraced a more radical perspective, believing that a radical transformation of capitalism was a serious alternative. I also saw this transformation as a process in which a radicalized labor movement led by revolutionary socialists would increasingly challenge corporations and eventually have the power and unity to transform and overthrow capitalism. This would then lay the basis for a society in which a multiracial working class would implement a participatory economic and political democracy based on the satisfaction of human needs and the full development of each person.

While I still believe very strongly in the need for building a democratic mass movement for radical change, I'm less certain about how that change will be enacted, by whom, and with what results. I'm now much more focused on the obstacles to radical change (including those identified by Buddhists), and the difficulty in identifying appropriate strategies and tactics in specific historical moments and eras. I've also sharpened my sense of the ways in which capitalism and other forms of systemic oppression reinforce each other in complex ways. And finally, I now believe there is not one theory or strategy that provides all the answers. We need to see radical change as encompassing a variety of perspectives and movements, and utilizing a range of strategies in a coordinated way. For example, Erik Olin Wright insightfully explored key strategic logics for challenging capitalism in his *How to Be an Anti-capitalist in the 21st Century*.[101] Deepak Bhargava and Stephanie Luce's, *Practical Radicals: Seven Strategies to Change the World* unfurls another recent example of such an approach. Their seven strategies range from bottom-up mass militant campaigns to electoral change efforts. Bhargava and Luce argue that, 'transformational change requires a mixture of creative strategies, working together harmoniously'.[102] I'm interested in the Left developing such a pluralistic approach, one that emerges from shared struggles and a continuing comradely debate marked by mutual respect and open-mindedness.

Chapter 6: **Rethinking Left Politics**

Reflections on a problematic model

The following reflections are based not only on a period of intensive participation with one Left group when I was much younger, but also the many experiences I've had with a range of Left organizations in coalitions and campaigns throughout my adult life, mostly as an independent activist. They also draw on conversations with friends and comrades about their experiences with the Left, and a continuing interest in autobiographies that feature valuable critical self-assessments of the Left.

I've never been involved in political groups that exhibited the worst symptoms of dysfunctional Left politics and attracted the most attention: the dominance of a leader or leadership clique; the demand for unquestioning agreement with all the group's principles, strategies, and tactics; an internal regime of personal abuse and degradation; and a kind of cut-throat, do or die competition with other Left groups. I have avoided such groups through good fortune, but also through my recoil from orthodoxies and demands to slavishly obey leaders.

As I noted in the Preface, the first Left group I joined was the New American Movement (NAM), an organization that emerged out of the dissolution of Students for a Democratic Society (SDS) in the early 1970s. After we disbanded our local NAM chapter, some of us decided to join the International Socialists (IS), a small group which was rooted in a dissident version of Trotskyism. The IS advocated a Third Camp socialism which viewed both the USA and the Soviet Union as societies in which a ruling class exploited and oppressed workers. The IS stood for revolutionary change but emphasized that socialism could only be created through a mass, democratic revolution. An influential founder of this political tendency, Hal Draper, called this stance 'socialism from below' and opposed both communist and reformist socialist parties because each, in their own way, had a top-down, bureaucratic conception of radical change.[103] For the IS, political parties were essential in offering strategies and leadership, but it was the workers themselves that must make and lead the revolution.

The IS was, in the context of the numerous Left groups which existed at this time, serious and reasonable in their approach. The organization encouraged robust, comradely debate on all key issues and had a collective leadership that worked well together. It encouraged the group's members to develop themselves politically and become leaders. No one felt unsafe to present their own views. Based on their particular brand of Left politics and their organizational approach, the IS did play an important role in the labor movement, helping to create and build several rank-and-file movements as part of an overall strategy of radicalizing unions. Even today, over 40 years later, the IS's notion of bottom-up workers' activity continues to be influential in the union movement and the Left, as well as in several important unions in the USA, including the International Brotherhood of Teamsters (IBT) and the United Auto Workers (UAW). In recent years DSA has embraced a rank and file strategy as the cornerstone of its work within the labor movement.

A few years after I joined the IS, however, the organization was in turmoil and declining due to ideological splits and setbacks in key areas of activity. The IS eventually merged with a few other small groups to form a new group – Solidarity – which still exists but remains quite small. To the extent that the group has any impact, it is primarily through individuals associated with Solidarity who work in the labor movement and academia. As an organization, it is unlikely to play a leading role in a revived Left.

The most important factor in its stunted growth was largely beyond the control of the IS and any other Left group. In the late 1970s and early 1980s, the economic and political conditions worked against radical movements. Neoliberalism – an economic model based on an updated version of laissez-faire capitalism and a set of pro-business/anti-labor public policies – became hegemonic throughout the capitalist world of the Global North. In the USA and the UK, the neoliberal political project received powerful support as President Ronald Reagan and Prime Minister Margaret Thatcher worked to destroy the welfare state and a regulated form of capitalism by breaking unions and shredding the social safety net.

Chapter 6: **Rethinking Left Politics**

They enacted laws and pursued policies which substantially reduced regulations and controls on corporations, expanded free trade deals, limited workers' rights, and cut government spending on education, health care, and income support for the poor. In both countries, the political consensus moved to the right and the insurgent movements from the 1960s faced a fierce pushback.

At the same time, employers deployed a variety of strategies to weaken the labor movement, particularly in manufacturing – outsourcing work to countries with low labor costs, demanding concessions from unions in contract negotiations, and implementing massive layoffs. As the industrial sector shrank drastically, and union leaders responded timidly to employers' demands for concessions, the very unions which the IS saw as the kernel of the labor movement and the basis for a radical transformation, were seriously weakened. Workers and their unions found themselves on the defensive. The IS and other Left groups had believed that there would be a continuing upsurge in mass movements and challenges to the neoliberal order. But the opposite occurred; the emergence of neoliberalism in the late 1970s ushered in a period of labor decline and a growing right-wing movement which not only attacked unions but other progressive movements as well. While the 2008 global financial collapse shook the ideological supremacy of neoliberalism, the basic architecture of the global economy continues to rest on neoliberal principles and assumptions.

The consolidation of neoliberal hegemony created huge obstacles for radical movements, and largely explains the collapse and continuing eclipse of the IS and other Left groups. However, two basic but problematic assumptions about radical politics and the role of activists in organizations have also had a serious impact. For the most part they go unchallenged, in spite of their debilitating influence on the functioning of Left organizations.

The first faulty assumption is that a group's effectiveness depends on whether it espouses the 'correct' theory and strategies. There is no complexity, uncertainty, or indeterminacy involved here. Instead of recognizing that a fruitful set of theories and practices emerge from dialogue between several perspectives, a binary division between a right and a wrong way of seeing and acting in the world holds sway. Left groups often compete with each other over who has the one true approach. Theoretical debates become quite heated as each group puts forward its particular perspective. At times these debates, which can extend to strategy and tactics, attain a level of abstraction reminiscent of medieval theological arguments over how many angels can dance on the head of a pin.

Here we see the same phenomenon that Bhikkhu Analayo analyzed in his discussion of the superiority conceit in relation to Buddhist lineages that I mentioned in Chapter 3. Each Left group develops a sense of ownership of, a closely held attachment to, their own approach. This is almost always harmful. Supposed ownership of the 'right line' closes a group off from other perspectives, and locks in a particular theory and practice. At the same time, the attachment to a particular perspective and set of strategies means that if the results are not what were expected, demoralization and disillusionment set in, and internal conflicts follow.

The IS was one of the groups that tried to be more open-minded and welcomed dialogue on the Left but it, too, largely accepted this assumption. Attachment to the particular theories and strategies which defined the group, as well as failures in practice, contributed to members becoming disoriented and demoralized when conditions gave the lie to our theoretical assumptions. As with many Left groups, we tended to assign blame for our failure to get good results, rather than engage in a process of open dialogue and assessment.

The other self-defeating assumption common in Left groups concerns the model of the dedicated political activist. Ironically, it draws on the model of human existence on which mainstream economics (and thus neoliberalism itself) rests: *homo economicus* (economic man), the rational pursuer of his wants and needs. As Marx and many others have pointed out, this model caricatures actual human beings, suppressing the full range of our capacities and interests – our affective lives above all – to justify capitalist hegemony.

According to the homo economicus model, human beings are essentially rational maximizers of their economic needs and wants. Full stop. In much

Chapter 6: Rethinking Left Politics

the same way, the model of human beings in radical politics involves a similar flattening and simplification. But rather than the rational calculator of benefits and costs in the market, *homo radical politicus* (excuse the mashup of Latin and English) applies her or his rationality and agency to social transformation. Thus, a radical activist is fully committed to political activity, faithfully carries out the decisions of the political group, and is willing to put aside all personal interests in pursuit of the cause. The radical activist focuses solely on political theory and the practical actions that the theory mandates. Relationships between group members restrict themselves to exchanging political views and figuring out which actions to take. Those who excel at these tasks and are the most effective and aggressive in presenting the group's 'right line', provide the exemplars for the group. Their skill at argumentation, rationality, courage, and dedication define them.

This model has its roots in the way that revolutionary groups in Russia and other countries functioned in the late 19th and early 20th centuries. Perhaps the most well-known exponent of homo radical politicus was Lenin, who in his struggles to gain dominance within the Russian revolutionary movement, argued that a successful political movement required a cadre of fully committed and politically correct activists The cadre compose the core of radical political groups. By the time I became active in the US Left in the early- and mid-1970s, this model of radical activism still held sway, and many Left groups presented themselves as the 'true' cadre organization.

The IS version of the cadre model had a more democratic tinge in that it made decisions about policies democratically to a large extent. Yet the cadre model of political activism in IS still curtailed the range of rank-and-file activities. If you wanted to make a serious commitment to the IS, you either worked full-time for the organization or, based on the IS's view that its crucial task was to help radicalize the labor movement, you dedicated yourself wholly and solely to organizing among workers to transform the most strategically powerful unions.

Today the cadre model has lost much of its prominence, but elements of homo radical politicus persist in Left groups. The essential skills and virtues of the radical activist remain argumentation, rationality, fearlessness in confronting the status quo, and total dedication to political activity.

What's missing here? What is left out? Our inner, personal life for starters – our emotions, our intimate and familial relationships, and our friendships have no role in this model. At the same time, the complex motivations and concerns that affect the relationships that we have with others go unrecognized, including our need for security and love, the prevalence of anger and envy when we feel harmed or disrespected, and the shifting patterns of status and interpersonal power in the way we actually live day to day. Further, the model suppresses any concerns about the great questions of life and death as extraneous 'spiritual' issues.

Finally, the model pays no attention to our vulnerability and limitations. It fails to recognize how little control we have over what happens in our life, and that our knowledge in any situation is almost always incomplete. In short, homo radical politicus excludes some of the most important aspects of a human life. It thereby ignores the way in which this exclusion of our inner lives has a crucial impact on the political movements that we create.

In this way the model promotes gendered notions of rationality and strength. Like the bodhisattva model we saw in Chapter 5, the paradigm is the heroic male. The radical activist is fiercely determined and undeterred by obstacles. He willingly goes up against powerful, even violent forces. He puts aside all other aspects of his life to fulfill his political duties, including his family and his own needs. And he knows how to get to the heart of the matter, to slice through confusions and falsehoods to identify and articulate the 'correct' view. Based on his willingness to fight against even the most powerful opponents, together with his piercing rationality and argumentative skills, he can function politically at the highest level. He is the political hero.

These stereotypically male qualities have been highly prized within the Left. Not surprisingly, male domination of Leftist groups has been widespread. Only in recent years has such domination met serious challenge. Yet, this gen-

Chapter 6: **Rethinking Left Politics**

dered model of political activism retains its hold. 'Mansplaining' endures, and women's voices and contributions tend to get short shrift. When women gain leadership positions within a Left organization, they come under pressure to conform to the model of homo radical politicus.

In these ways, this self-defeating model has contributed to many of the internal problems within Left groups. When we ignore important aspects of our lives – our limitations and vulnerability, our wide range of needs and interests, our tendency to react to perceived or real threats – we lose the ability to resolve the inevitable disagreements that political life throws up. For example, the drive for power and dominance, and our egotistical search for recognition and praise, often fuel political disputes. At the same time, if our capacity and need for compassion and care go unrecognized, then we'll probably fail to treat our comrades with mutual respect and kindness. We'll deny each other the support we need to deal with the risks and uncertainties of a life of political activism. Combined with the challenges we face in the 'external' political environment, the effects of this emotional and spiritual impoverishment have proved disastrous. Political debates turn vicious and lead to internal conflicts and splits; Left groups become undemocratic and hierarchical; and a sense of disillusionment and anger arises over mistreatment by others.

As I noted in Chapter 1, maintaining internal democratic structures and processes can limit these destructive tendencies and create a healthier organizational life. Leaders need to be accountable, and the group must foster an egalitarian culture. In recent years Left organizations have also come under pressure to provide a 'safe space' for activists; this change reflects a laudable concern about mistreatment and disrespect within a group, particularly when it's directed at people of color, women, and the LGBTQ community. However, the need for a safe space is often discussed in ways which can discourage robust debate, insofar as the primary objective is to protect individuals from words or actions that are deemed harmful. But what counts as harmful is often conceived of so broadly that any form of speech or action which creates a level of unease can become taboo. In this way genuine political debate can be inhibited, which in turn hampers efforts to generate viable strategies and identify goals. At the same time, the demand for safe spaces often assumes that human beings are essentially weak and passive, incapable of learning and developing from adversity.

How Buddhist insights and values can help sustain political activism

Putting aside conventional Buddhist notions of nirvana, karma, and supernatural entities, key insights and values shared by Buddhists offer valuable resources to address the Left's internal problems. In contrast to the impoverished view of human life that homo radical politicus infers, Buddhism can provide the Left with a fuller understanding of the needs, motivations, and tendencies of human beings, and how to address them. The Left also needs to embrace its ethic of care and compassion if we seek to develop a radical politics in which our means chime with our stated ends. Finally, Buddhism offers us an effective contemplative practice – mindfulness and other forms of meditation – to counteract the three destructive poisons of greed, anger, and delusion.

The three poisons form part of our biologically evolved human nature which we entrench in habits of behavior and thought. Buddhism teaches that we have the capacity to counter them by cultivating wisdom, meditative practices, and ethics. Wisdom exposes the causes of suffering and advances the remedy for mitigating suffering. Meditation generates mindfulness – the art of maintaining a non-reactive, moment-by-moment awareness of our thoughts, feelings, bodily sensations, and surrounding environment – and the ability to focus our minds in a tranquil, collected way. Buddhist ethics acknowledges the ways in which we interconnect to each other, and that we all suffer yet seek happiness. To reduce suffering and promote flourishing, Buddhism prioritizes the values of care and non-harming as the basis of an ethical life. In short, Buddhism's remedy for the three poisons is the cultivation of mindful awareness, understanding our interconnectedness, and being compassionate in everyday life.

Chapter 6: Rethinking Left Politics

So, how does this emphasis strengthen the work of political activists and the overall movement for social justice? Expanding on the arguments made by Travis Donoho in a recent article,[104] I suggest that meditation, the recognition of interconnection, and compassion facilitate our sustained activism in the following ways:

- ☆ By developing our capacity to be more mindful and non-reactive through meditation, we can deal with the ups and downs of movement activity, stay focused on our strategies and ultimate goals, and exercise patience and perseverance in our efforts.
- ☆ An awareness of our limitations, complexity and vulnerability enables us to have more compassion toward each other in political settings. We are all imperfect; we all have strengths and weaknesses. We all suffer in various ways, not just from social institutions but from the unskillful ways with which we relate to our experience. A recognition of these basic facts of human existence leads to a more realistic perspective on what we can accomplish together and how we can help each other.
- ☆ Buddhism's recognition of uncertainty and change promotes what the Zen teacher Shunryu Suzuki calls 'beginner's mind', an openness to new perspectives and a refusal to get too attached to any one point of view.[105] This promotes healthy debates and discussions among political comrades.
- ☆ Based on the notions of interdependence, impermanence/change, and compassion, Buddhism offers a worldview which complements a socialist economic model based on cooperation, democracy, and ecological sustainability.
- ☆ Buddhists understand that, given the interconnected and changing nature of life, we don't have complete control over events, and the results of our efforts are often not what we wished for. What we accomplish will depend on the efforts of our fellow activists and all the 'causes and conditions' that provide the context for our activity. At the

same time, when we lose sight of these insights and have an overly self-absorbed focus on *my* role and *my* efforts to achieve social change, we are likely to cause ourselves and others to suffer, to be harmed. In this context, we can easily lose sight of what our goals are.

☆ Recognizing our limits and lack of control, and the need to cultivate mindfulness and compassion, political activists recognize the importance of practices of self-care to sustain our political activism. Mushim Patricia Ikeda has emphasized the value of self-care and mindfulness in her *Great Vow for Mindful Activists*. She urges practitioners to reflect on the following: 'Aware of suffering and injustice, I am working to create a more just, peaceful, and sustainable world. I promise, for the benefit of all, to practice self-care, mindfulness, healing and joy. I vow to not burn out.'[106]

☆ While anger as a response to social injustice and harm is natural and understandable, and is an important impetus to engaging in radical politics, activism based mainly on hatred – particularly hatred toward our opponents – often attracts negative consequences. We can easily become overwhelmed by anger and give up on doing anything, or our activism can become less about an appropriate response and more about meeting our need to express that anger. We can learn to recognize the common humanity of our opponents on the field of conflict and not demonize them, while still being steadfast in our fight against their actions. We recognize that the capitalist system is our primary enemy, and that demonizing corporate leaders or those who support this system often drives away more potential allies than it attracts.

Buddhist insights practically applied: making meetings more useful and productive

How can we apply these insights and values in the day-to-day life of Left groups? Several areas of political activity invite the application of the Buddhist insights and values listed above, including the way in which political activists communicate their views to others (allies, opponents, etc.), how they frame salient issues, and determine which issues to highlight.

I'll take up one particularly crucial aspect of an activist's life: the meetings that we attend to discuss issues, evaluate and choose strategies, and identify our goals. Meetings of radical political activists often lead to frustration and reflect unhealthy relationships and dynamics in Left groups. Katya de Kadt has noted some of the typical problems:[107]

- ☆ meetings are often too long because much of the discussion is repetitive;
- ☆ people get wedded to their positions and don't take in what others are saying;
- ☆ at meetings, hurtful things are said to others, including unintentional slights;
- ☆ white people, particularly white men, often dominate the discussion in meetings;
- ☆ tensions and unresolved disputes often infuse meetings.

Along with establishing guidelines which encourage respectful discussion in which all are encouraged to participate, applying Buddhist insights regarding mindfulness, interconnection, and compassion in a realistic and appropriate way can overcome (or at least ameliorate) problematic aspects of meetings. These insights need to be incorporated before, during, and after meetings.

Before a meeting

Participating in a meeting in a productive way demands that we 'check our egos at the door' so we can work in a democratic and productive way with other participants. We need to size up what our actual contribution can be, and how we can foster a sense of teamwork and camaraderie. We need to be centered and authentic. We also need to be able to focus on our common objectives.

Although the following guidelines could help any meeting participant, leaders and meeting facilitators have a special obligation to prepare for meetings not just by developing agendas, but by bringing to mind their own attitudes, intentions, and feelings. Before coming to a meeting, each leader or facilitator should give themselves a few minutes to 'center' themselves and reflect what's about to take place. This checklist of practices and reflections will foster mindfulness and compassion before they participate in a meeting:

1. 'Check in' and center yourself. Sit quietly for a moment and take a few deep breaths. Then, ask yourself:
   - What am I feeling at this moment? Hope? Anxiety? Fear? Anticipation?
   - Is there tension in my body? Where? Breathe in and out slowly a few times...
   - Am I bringing any anger or resentment into this meeting? Why?
2. Reflect on the importance of contributing to a productive and respectful discussion at the meeting.
   - How can I make a positive contribution to this meeting?
   - What are the common needs and goals I share with other meeting participants?
   - Remember that my perspective and attitudes may not be shared by everyone else. Each of us is shaped by different experiences and identities.
   - Remember to distinguish disagreement with someone's view from anger at that person's character or nature.
3. Consider what you would like the meeting to accomplish. What would be a good result? But keep in mind the following:
   - We can rarely control the outcome of an activity.
   - Working together with others can often be difficult, even with everyone's best intentions.
   - Be grateful for any progress made during the meeting.

During a meeting

Many activist organizations, including DSA, have developed a set of community guidelines which lay out agreements on how group members should behave in a meeting.[108] In general, these guidelines aim to promote respectful discussions, inclusiveness, and kind speech. Incorporating mindfulness and compassion into the meeting process ensures that these guidelines are more than just words on paper. Rather than just note their existence, the meeting facilitator should discuss the guidelines with the participants and emphasize the following points:

- ☆ We are all together in a common struggle and goal, whatever our different views, experiences, and groups that we belong to.
- ☆ None of us is perfect or has all the right answers. We have to help each other out.
- ☆ How we treat each other at the meeting should exemplify the kind of society we want to create – participatory, inclusive, respectful, and democratic.

If appropriate, the facilitator might include a moment or two of silence to reflect on these points before proceeding to other agenda items. In the body of the meeting, facilitators should gently intervene if community agreements are not being followed, and remind people of their importance. At the end of the meeting, the facilitator should check in with the participants to find out how they're feeling, especially about the meeting process.

After a meeting

Leaders and meeting facilitators typically discuss how meetings have gone as part of an ongoing assessment of projects and activities, in regularly scheduled leadership meetings. In some cases, there will be a formal debrief which examines in some detail various aspects of the meeting. Such discussions should also include consideration of the *process* of the meeting. Did the participants abide by the community rules of agreement? And did the meeting help to:

- ☆ Foster a sense of connection and community among the participants?
- ☆ Expand participation by individuals and groups that had been less involved or perhaps marginalized?
- ☆ Highlight the common objectives and goals of participants?
- ☆ Cultivate tolerance, openness, and mutual respect?

In addition, each leader and facilitator should take a few minutes to make their own assessment of the meeting – not just the results of the meeting and the items listed above, but their own role in the meeting. In this regard here are some important points to reflect on:

- ☆ What was my role during the meeting? Did I play a constructive role?
- ☆ Did I exemplify the guidelines for a respectful discussion?
- ☆ Did difficult feelings come up for me during the meeting? Was I aware of them during the meeting? How did I respond?
- ☆ Do I need to change the way I interacted with others?

Secular, radically engaged Buddhists and the Left

These suggestions for how political activists can incorporate mindfulness and compassion into their participation in meetings represent just one way in which Buddhist insights and values can help sustain activism and promote a healthier organizational culture. As I've indicated above, Buddhism has much to offer in other areas, and we should explore them as well. Through an emphasis on mindfulness, compassion, and a recognition of our interconnectedness, secular, radically engaged Buddhists can play a role in helping political movements avoid some of the pervasive pitfalls of Left groups – membership burnout, organizational dysfunction, and debilitating internal disputes. The success of political movements depends on their programs and policies. Creating and maintaining organizations which embody relevant Buddhist insights and values is no less important, of course.

At this point, I don't see the usefulness or practicality of creating a separate organization of secular, radically engaged Buddhists to promote these insights and values within the Left. A more useful and feasible alternative would be for those of us who share this perspective to bring into the existing groups and movements we support a sensibility and modus operandi which foregrounds mindfulness and compassion. As part of our involvement in the Left, we can interact with others in a mindful and compassionate way. In this way we bring and instill a model of political activism which engenders more respectful and compassionate interactions among group members. We can also help movements avoid behaviors and actions that feed off ego-driven rage and fear.

Finally, we can be part of the process, helping the Left make changes in organizational functioning that facilitate communication, democracy, and mutual respect. In all these ways, secular, radically engaged Buddhists can play a crucial role as a 'mindfulness and compassion' tendency within a revitalized Left.

Left politics in a complex world

The need for Buddhist insights and values – mindfulness, compassion, an ethics of care, a sense of openness to change and uncertainty, and a recognition of human vulnerability and limits – has grown today as Left activists face a challenging and complex environment. When socialism, communism, and anarchism emerged as significant political movements in the 19th century and as they developed through the 20th century, the central challenge for the Left stood out: to unite the working class into a powerful and politically conscious movement capable of transforming the capitalist system.

This task remains relevant. Now, however, we have come to understand that neoliberal capitalism is a much more complex system in its internal dynamics and its capacity to respond to progressive movements. The Left has tended to see the development of capitalism in terms of a set of simple, binary alternatives: reform or revolution or, in the stark terms posed by Rosa Luxemburg during the first world war: socialism or barbarism.[109] As capitalism has developed in the late 20th and early 21st centuries, we now know that these binaries don't necessarily capture the full range of possibilities. For example, in analyzing the current internal problems and crises of the capitalist system, Wolfgang Streeck rejects the notion that the end of capitalism will involve an apocalyptic event – either a worldwide revolution or a collapse into barbarism. Instead, he sees the ending of capitalism as an extended process in which a 'multiplicity of infirmities each of which will be all the more untreatable'[110] degrades the system. In his view, the slow decline of capitalism goes hand in hand with the fragmentation of the working class and forecloses any chance of a collective challenge to the system.

I question Streeck's view that we have seen the end of organized opposition to capitalism, that working people and others have become so disorganized and demoralized that radical social transformation is impossible. Since Streeck wrote his book in 2016, there have been significant workers' protests and strikes throughout the world, as well as the development of other insurgent movements, including the Black Lives Matter protests that erupted worldwide in the wake of George Floyd's murder by the police in Minneapolis, Minnesota. Still, if Streeck's pessimism about collective action may be unwarranted, his analysis of capitalism does point to the complex ways in which the system has mutated, and the need to avoid simplistic, dualistic scenarios.

Moreover, while even the earliest Left movements recognized the importance of understanding and fighting for groups which experience oppression and discrimination based on race, gender, ethnicity, nationality, and religion, the main focus of the Left's analysis and strategy was the workplace and the economy, as this was seen as the main arena of conflict and social transformation. The Left saw other, 'extra-economic' struggles around oppression as significant but conceptually distinct, secondary to the primary struggle between the working class and capital. That view has begun to change in recent years, and it's become increasingly clear that we cannot understand capitalism as a system without including as essential elements of our analysis precisely those forms of oppression which are not based on class exploitation per se. In her book *Cannibal Capitalism*, Nancy Fraser presents just such an approach.

Chapter 6: **Rethinking Left Politics**

She argues for:

> Expanding our view of capitalism to include extra-economic ingredients of capitalism's diet, it brings together in a single frame *all* the oppressions, contradictions, and conflicts of the present conjuncture. In this frame, structural injustice means capitalist exploitation, to be sure, but also gender domination, and racial/imperial oppression—both non-accidental by-products of a societal order that subordinates social reproduction to commodity production and that demands racialized expropriation to underwrite profitable exploitation. As understood here, likewise, the system's contradictions incline it not only to economic crises but also crises of care, ecology, and politics, all of which are in full flower today, courtesy of the long spell of corporate bingeing known as neoliberalism.[111]

The formidable task of developing a comprehensive analysis of neoliberal capitalism and a strategy for its radical transformation extends to other factors with destructive impacts, some of which have emerged since Marx's time. The climate emergency heads this list, the outcome of neoliberal capitalism's accelerated drive to concentrate global wealth and power in the hands of a tiny minority. How do we connect the existential struggle to stop fossil fuel emissions with the need for radical change? What do we make of the degrowth trend, whose advocates argue that we need to make fundamental changes in our patterns of consumption?

Beyond the climate emergency lie the various aspects of neoliberalism that profoundly shape our sense of self and tie us more deeply into the system as isolated, passive individuals: mass consumerism, the ubiquity of advertising, the use of credit cards and debt to finance purchases, constant stimulation from TV, cable, and social media, and the massive amount of mis- and disinformation.

To understand and respond wisely to our contemporary world, Left activists must break out of standard conceptual schemes, consider other perspectives, and embrace a comprehensive world view. Buddhism offers the Left important resources in this context. The Left would do well to adopt the Buddhist emphasis on open-mindedness, its admonition to hold views lightly, and to acknowledge our shared human vulnerability and limitations. In this way the Left can play a positive role in reducing suffering and creating a society in which everyone has the opportunity to flourish.

Part 3
A Flourishing Life for All

Chapter 7
Human Flourishing

You may have noticed that I have used the words 'flourish' and 'flourishing' in this book frequently. To be exact, these terms have appeared 76 times so far! I have often paired these words with the 'reduction of suffering' as I've explored the key elements and goals of a secular, radically engaged Buddhist perspective. Clearly, then, the notion of flourishing is crucial to my approach, but what does it mean to flourish in life? How do individuals flourish? And what kind of society are we trying to build which offers the opportunity for all of us to flourish, not just as part of a small minority which has the resources, income, and power to get what they want in life? After offering a critique of the theory and practice of mainstream Buddhism and Left politics in the previous chapters, I now want to focus on a positive vision of the life that a secular, radical Buddhist approach entails. In this chapter I discuss the notion of flourishing itself; in the next chapter I'll lay out the key tasks and tenets of someone committed to individual and social transformation.

The notion of human flourishing takes pride of place for those of us who are attempting to develop a secular, radically engaged approach to the dharma, which itself tackles the systemic roots of suffering. In part, we emphasize the notion of flourishing as an alternative to what most Buddhists view as their highest individual goal: the end of suffering through the attainment of nirvana.

Secular Buddhists (whether radically engaged or not) question or reject the idea of nirvana as a realm or state of being beyond the natural world in which we live, as well as the belief that the attainment of nirvana in this form results in a permanent and complete liberation from all forms of suffering. The goal for secular Buddhists is instead the lessening of the various forms of suffering that we experience, and the cultivation of human capacities that underpin a full, satisfying, and meaningful life in this world. Our highest good, the *summum bonum*, is thus a world in which everyone has the opportunity and capacity to live a full, satisfying life even though we inevitably experience pain, loss and suffering as part of our human condition.

Some secular Buddhists, including Stephen Batchelor, retain the notion of nirvana as the freedom from reactivity (the various forms of clinging) for moments or periods in this life. For Batchelor, awareness of nirvana is the third of the four tasks:

> Here one becomes aware of nirvana whenever one understands reactivity for what it is and thereby gains freedom from its control. In this case the experience of nirvana becomes possible even while in the throes of reactivity. ... To behold and thus become aware of nirvana means to consciously affirm and valorize those moments when you see for yourself that you are free to think, speak, and act in ways that are not determined by reactivity. ... Nirvana is clearly visible the moment reactivity stops.[112]

While Batchelor has developed this further in the concept of the 'everyday sublime', others have also adopted this perspective and see 'nirvanic moments' as a crucial element of a flourishing life.

For my part, I would rather use other terms to describe our experiences of life when reactivity has been substantially lessened and we are mindfully present. While the details vary to some extent, the core elements of this type of experience can be found in Maslow's notion of peak experiences,[113] Csíkszentmihályi's theory of flow states,[114] and Tara Brach's concept of the release from what she describes as 'the trance of unworthiness'.[115] However, whether we retain the term nirvana in this sense or not, the main point is that human

Chapter 7: **Human Flourishing**

flourishing – not nirvana in the traditional sense – is the goal toward which our overall practice as secular Buddhists is directed.

Yet, despite the ubiquity of the term human flourishing in secular Buddhist discussions, this notion still calls for detailed explanation. We hear talk about certain capacities of humans being essential to flourishing but what are they? What are the conditions for human flourishing? How is flourishing at an individual level related to creating a society in which all human beings can flourish? Can an individual still flourish if they have suffered harm and been deprived of their basic needs?

To craft a viable notion of human flourishing, one that recognizes human complexity, we need to bring together several perspectives that offer insights into the human condition and our capabilities. Seth Zuihō Segall, a Zen Buddhist teacher who advocates a naturalistic approach to Buddhism, has taken this approach in his recent book. In *Buddhism and Human Flourishing*, Segall presents a theory of human flourishing – what he calls a 'eudaimonic model of enlightenment' – which integrates Aristotle's perspective on human virtues with aspects of the Buddhist path. (I will introduce the ancient Greek concept of eudaimonia below.) His ten-attribute model of eudaimonic enlightenment synthesizes four key components:

- ☆ modern western Buddhist teachings concerning the amelioration of suffering and the moderation of desire;
- ☆ traditional Buddhist teachings regarding not-self, emptiness, and duality;
- ☆ a revised Buddhist-Aristotelian list of virtues; and
- ☆ a recognition of the importance of participating in the civic life of one's community.[116]

In what follows, I take a similar, synthetic approach, but the human flourishing I propose includes a radical, emancipatory dimension, and links flourishing to internal and external causes and conditions. As part of developing an account of what it means to live a full, meaningful, and deeply satisfactory life – that is, to flourish – we need to incorporate Marx's view of human nature, which emphasizes creative, productive labor at the heart of human flourishing; and Martha Nussbaum's 'capabilities' approach, which identifies a set of conditions and capacities essential for a rich human life. Bringing these perspectives into a dialogue with Buddhist insights will, I believe, help us develop a more adequate understanding of human flourishing.

Aristotle, eudaimonia, and a 'near enemy'

The modern notion of human flourishing derives from the concept of eudaimonia – a prominent term in ancient Greek moral philosophy, particularly Aristotle's. Eudaimonia denotes a state of human flourishing or well-being in which we achieve a state of 'true' or 'real' happiness or fulfillment, the sort of happiness worth seeking or having. It is happiness one enjoys when we express our unique human capacities and live in an ethical and meaningful way.

Aristotle held that everything that exists, including human beings and other forms of life, have a telos or final purpose based on their unique nature. A knife's telos is fulfilled if the knife can cut certain materials easily. The telos of a tree is to develop into its mature, structural form and produce fruit, nuts, or flowers, as well as reproduce. Under the right conditions, a plant, animal, or a human being can progress toward their unique telos and achieve the best form of life possible for them.

But what is the telos of human beings? What makes human beings unique and distinct from other life forms? While we share with other animals many capacities, according to Aristotle, our capacity for reason, and using that capacity to guide our lives, distinguishes human beings. If we apply reason well, then we are living fully as human beings. But the appropriate use of reason depends on the cultivation of certain virtues. Real happiness consists in taking part in virtuous activities inspired and guided by reason.

Here is how Aristotle identified the distinctive nature and telos of human beings' life activity in the *Nicomachean Ethics*:

Chapter 7: **Human Flourishing**

So whatever, then, would this work be? For living appears to be something common even to plants, but what is peculiar [to human beings] is [1098a] being sought. One must set aside, then, the life characterized by nutrition as well as growth ... if the work of a human being is an activity of soul in accord with reason, or not without reason ... and we posit the work of a human being as a certain life, and this is an activity of soul and actions accompanied by reason, the work of a serious man being to do these things well and nobly, and each thing is brought to completion well in accord with the virtue proper to it—if this is so, then the human good becomes an activity of soul in accord with virtue, and if there are several virtues, then in accord with the best and most complete one.[117]

Aristotle viewed a flourishing life as one in which, based on our capacity for reason, we develop certain moral and intellectual virtues, contemplate the truth, and participate as citizens in a political community to further the social good. Aristotle identified a long list of important moral virtues, among which are courage, temperance, magnanimity, and justice. His intellectual virtues span a range of human cognitive capacities: knowledge of craft, scientific understanding, *phronesis* or practical wisdom, and philosophical wisdom. Cultivating these virtues serves our telos, enabling us to progress toward a state of eudaimonia, or flourishing.

Aristotle's account of human flourishing is based on what he believed to be an objective understanding of the unique qualities of human beings. We have the capacity to flourish because of who we essentially are. This view differs markedly from today's popular conception of happiness which highlights our subjective experiences of pleasure and pain.

For many people, happiness is about getting what we want, enjoying the maximum amount of pleasure, and having a lot of things that we own that we can use or display. It's having the experience of feeling pleasure and enjoyment most of the time; and those who can accumulate the maximum amount of such experiences in a lifetime have led the happiest life. Or, as a bumper sticker in the 1980s declared: 'He who dies with the most toys wins!' The notion that the goal of life is to accumulate pleasurable experiences and objects reflects a selfish individualism that permeates capitalist society. This view of a happy life contradicts Aristotle's notion of flourishing as a way of life which is deeply ethical and meaningful.

Human flourishing is sometimes confused with a 'near enemy' of eudaimonia. During the 1960s, countercultural circles and some versions of humanistic psychotherapy traced our problems and suffering in life back to restrictive social and cultural norms which repressed our natural capacities. The key to happiness, according to this view, lies in freeing ourselves from those norms so we can fully express ourselves, no longer inhibited or uptight – in short, actualizing all our capacities by 'letting it all hang out'.

While human flourishing as eudaimonia does entail the expression or actualization of certain capacities, a eudaimonic perspective distinguishes between capacities which contribute to flourishing and those that don't. (Buddhism makes the same distinction between skillful and unskillful thoughts, emotions, words, and actions.) For example, we have the biologically-evolved capacity for rage and destructive competition, but we also have the capacity to love, cooperate, and help each other out. All these capacities constitute our complex make-up. While a secular, radically engaged Buddhist places a positive value on the capacities essential to human fulfillment and happiness, they don't constitute our 'true nature' or 'basic goodness' in comparison to capacities which cause suffering.

Any theory of human flourishing thus must include an account of human beings which recognizes the full range of our capacities and behaviors, and criteria for determining which of those capacities contribute to living a meaningful, genuinely fulfilling life. But those criteria must inevitably include an ethical or moral component based on what counts as a 'good' or 'skillful' life. Of course, opinions will vary on this topic. Flourishing is not a value-neutral concept.

Chapter 7: **Human Flourishing**

Marx on human flourishing

Aristotle's vision of a flourishing life, based on our capacity for reason, drew on the kind of culture he lived in and his social status in it. The intellectual and moral virtues on which he based his ideal of a flourishing life were those of the aristocratic class which governed that society. The virtues of philosophical contemplation, practical wisdom (the ability to find the correct course of action in each specific situation), and civic engagement marked out a good life for those who did not perform manual labor and had the leisure to contemplate, discuss and formulate public policy.

As valuable as Aristotle's concept of eudaimonia is, we need to include additional elements that address those of us who work, at home and away, to sustain our daily lives. Aristotle's vision of a good life lacks this crucial dimension, which Marx focused on in his own contribution to the idea of the good life.

Like Aristotle, Marx worked from a theory of human nature and flourishing that pinpointed a uniquely human element. For Aristotle, it is reason; for Marx – writing at the dawn of industrial capitalism and the expansion of commerce – it is our capacity for creative, productive labor, or *praxis*. When we interact with our environment to meet our needs (for food, shelter, clothing and so on), we change ourselves, our relationships with others, and our environment in the process. Although the capacity for self-conscious, goal-directed activity (praxis) inheres in each individual, that capacity can only be actualized in a social context. Productivity depends on cooperation, Marx insisted. Thus praxis takes the form of social labor: the cooperative process whereby we interact with nature and each other to meet our material needs and wants. Discussing the unique transformative and self-transformative character of human labor, Marx notes that:

> Labour is, in the first place a process in which both man and
> Nature participate, and in which man of his own accord starts,
> regulates, and controls the material re-actions between himself

and Nature. He opposes himself to Nature as one of his own forces, setting in motion arms and legs, head and hands, the natural forces of his body, in order to appropriate Nature's productions in a form adapted to his own wants. By thus acting on the external world and changing it, he at the same time changes his own nature. He develops his slumbering powers and compels them to act in obedience to his sway.[118]

David Leopold emphasizes the central role that Marx's notion of human flourishing, based on praxis, plays in his radical, emancipatory theory. Marx based his critique of capitalism not just on its internal contradictions and exploitation of workers, but on its denial of a flourishing life for the vast majority. A capitalist society prevents people from actualizing their unique human capacity. As Leopold writes:

> This model of human flourishing ... provides a normative framework for both the critique of existing class-divided societies, and the construction of a rational and humane alternative. There is little doubt about the strength and extent of Marx's anger at the ways in which the existing world frustrates human flourishing; the contemporary organization of work, for instance, is said to produce 'stunted monsters' rather than fully human beings. In contrast, in the humane and rational (communist) future, he suggests that individuals will finally become 'species beings'—that is, they will actualize their essential human powers in their 'empirical life'.[119]

According to Marx, in a non-exploitative, democratic, and cooperative society, human beings will be able express our essential powers in work and other spheres of life. Under communism, new technologies will enable us to reduce the workday and give us more time for other activities. Once freed from alienated labor, and with more time to develop our talents, human life can truly flourish.

While Marx denounced pie-in-the-sky utopianism, and left no blueprint for a communist society, he offered us a vision of an unalienated, flourishing life in a cooperative society in which people can express themselves in a myriad of positive ways. In such a society, human beings will be able to engage in productive and creative activities both in paid employment and in their leisure time. Instead of being forced to assume one role in a capitalist-controlled division of labor, we'll actualize our talents and interests in a variety of areas.[120]

For Marx, human flourishing encompasses both unalienated, productive labor and intellectual activity. Though he recognized a broader set of arenas in which we can express our human powers, he focused on praxis in the form of social labor. This focus leaves out some essential areas of human experience and activity, including those dimensions of human life that our patriarchal culture assigns to women: emotions, caretaking, and social relationships.

Nussbaum and the capabilities approach

As part of her effort to provide a normative standard for evaluating whether societies and countries are socially just and provide opportunities for a good life, the American philosopher Martha Nussbaum has developed the 'capabilities approach' in dialogue with the economist Amartya Sen. This perspective helps us develop a richer sense of human flourishing.

The ability to pursue a dignified or flourishing life calls for more than freedom *from* exploitation or oppression at the hands of the government or private organizations, Nussbaum argues. To flourish, we need to be able to exercise our human potential in a range of life activities; and this freedom requires a broad range of social structures and public policies to support individuals' right *to* flourish. Acknowledging Marx's contribution to the issue, Nussbaum offers a concise summary of her approach in these terms:

> The basic idea of my version of the capabilities approach ... is that we begin with a conception of the dignity of the human being, and

of a life that is worthy of that dignity—a life that has available in it 'truly human functioning,' in the sense described by Marx in his 1844 *Economic and Philosophical Manuscripts*. With this basic idea as a starting point, I then attempt to justify a list of ten capabilities as central requirements of a life with dignity. These ten capabilities ... are part of a minimum account of social justice: a society that does not guarantee these to all its citizens, at some appropriate threshold level, falls short of being a fully just society, whatever its level of opulence. Moreover, the capabilities are held to be important for each and every person: each person is treated as an end, and none as a mere adjunct or means to the ends of others.[121]

Nussbaum's list of the central human capabilities as elements of a flourishing life spans the full range of human experience, from the physical and affective dimensions of our existence, to our cognitive and creative faculties, to our social engagement on interpersonal, work, and society-wide levels. Her list is composed of:

1. **Life**. Being able to live to the end of a human life of normal length; not dying prematurely, or before one's life is so reduced as to be not worth living.
2. **Bodily Health.** Being able to have good health, including reproductive health; to be adequately nourished; to have adequate shelter.
3. **Bodily Integrity.** Being able to move freely from place to place; to be secure against violent assault, including sexual assault and domestic violence; having opportunities for sexual satisfaction and for choice in matters of reproduction.
4. **Senses, Imagination, and Thought.** Being able to use the senses, to imagine, think, and reason – and to do these things in a 'truly

Chapter 7: **Human Flourishing**

human' way, a way informed and cultivated by an adequate education, including, but by no means limited to, literacy and basic mathematical and scientific training.

5. **Emotions.** Being able to have attachments to things and people outside ourselves; to love those who love and care for us, to grieve at their absence; in general, to love, to grieve, to experience longing, gratitude, and justified anger.
6. **Practical Reason.** Being able to form a conception of the good and to engage in critical reflection about the planning of one's life.
7. **Affiliation.**
   A. Being able to live with and toward others, to recognize and show concern for other human beings, to engage in various forms of social interaction; to be able to imagine the situation of another.
   B. Having the social bases of self-respect and nonhumiliation; being able to be treated as a dignified being whose worth is equal to that of others.
8. **Other Species.** Being able to live with concern for and in relation to animals, plants, and the world of nature.
9. **Play.** Being able to laugh, to play, to enjoy recreational activities.
10. **Control Over One's Environment.**
    A. Political. Being able to participate effectively in political choices that govern one's life; having the right of political participation, protections of free speech and association.
    B. Material. Being able to hold property (both land and movable goods), and having property rights on an equal basis with others; having the right to seek employment on an equal basis with others; having the freedom from unwarranted search and seizure. In work, being able to work as a human being, exercising practical reason, and entering into meaningful relationships of mutual

recognition with other workers.[122]

Nussbaum's capabilities approach helps us to flesh out a more rounded notion of human flourishing. First, her list of capabilities reflects a broad range of human capacities and experiences. She doesn't just highlight rationality or creativity as essential aspects of human nature but identifies the many and various ways in which we relate to the world. Further, for each of the capabilities she names, there is a corresponding set of social norms, economic resources, and public policies which allow an individual to actualize that aspect of human flourishing. For example, with respect to securing her 7B above – 'having the social bases of self-respect and nonhumiliation' – she calls for strong cultural, social, legal, and political institutions which support nondiscrimination with respect to race, gender, sexual orientation, religion, and so on. In formulating a normative standard for social justice, she emphasizes the social, political, and economic preconditions for human flourishing.

Internal and external conditions for human flourishing

Each in their own way – Nussbaum and Marx – demonstrate how human flourishing depends on social arrangements which enable each individual to actualize those capacities which contribute to flourishing. We might call these social arrangements the 'external' conditions for flourishing. On the other hand, in Buddhist circles, the emphasis tends to be on the need for each individual to cultivate certain internal conditions for a flourishing life or, in the case of traditional Buddhists, as elements of the path that leads to nirvana. These internal conditions arise when we cultivate the three main facets of life covered by the eightfold path: meditative practices such as mindfulness and concentration, an ethical life centered on the values of care and compassion, and an appropriate understanding of reality (that is, wisdom). According to ancestral Buddhism, if we fully develop these capacities, then we can experience a good and happy life irrespective of the external conditions that we face. The goal of Buddhist practice is often framed as the experience of peace, freedom, and happiness under any conditions.

This is surely a noble aspiration. Even the most privileged individuals

Chapter 7: **Human Flourishing**

can't avoid life's difficult contingencies: a racist, xenophobic, and lying demagogue is elected president; our child suffers from a severe illness; we are mistreated and disrespected on the basis of our race or gender; we are forced to work in a job that pays inadequate wages and offers little room for autonomy; a lab test indicates a serious problem in our health, and so on. The four painful aspects of the 'eight worldly winds', as listed in an early Buddhist text, the Lokavipatti Sutta (AN 8.6) – pain, loss, disrepute, and blame – are an inevitable part of each life.[123] Mindfulness, compassion, and wisdom cannot erase these realities, but they allow us to meet them with some measure of equanimity.

The three pillars of the Buddhist path are important for other reasons. If flourishing draws on the actualization of certain human capacities, we must be able to harmonize their expression and avoid getting overly attached to a particular dimension of human experience. Mindfulness, compassion, and wisdom provide us with the internal resources to do so. Our finite lives and limited personal opportunities stop us from actualizing ourselves in every dimension of human life. We need to make choices all the time about which aspects of life are the most important to us and demand more time, attention, and energy at any particular stage.

At the same time, mindfulness, compassion, and wisdom can help us avoid getting too attached to a particular kind of experience. For example, Nussbaum highlights the capacity to have strong emotional attachments, to love and be loved, as essential to human flourishing. Yet we tend to cling to or reject such experiences depending on whether we experience them as pleasant or unpleasant. The appropriate internal conditions allow us to relate to these experiences in a more skillful way – appreciating and enjoying our relationships without attaching to them, recognizing unpleasant experiences as an inevitable part of life's impermanence.

Similarly, Nussbaum argues that our ability to participate in political choices that govern our lives is a precondition for human flourishing. We need a voice in determining the social and political structures in which we live. This requirement extends to political activism aimed at transforming unjust structures. As I noted in the previous chapter, though, we must find a mindful, wise, and compassionate approach to political activity. With this sort of approach, we can commit ourselves to campaigns that will transform external conditions and achieve social justice without giving way to ego-driven anger at our perceived enemies or expecting that we'll always meet with success. With the right internal conditions, our political activity becomes more effective. They also help us to avoid burnout and to sustain our activism in the long term.

That said, we should avoid the error of ignoring or trivializing the impact of external conditions on our ability to live a good life. One of my dharma buddies once posed the following provocative question during a discussion on this issue: Can a mother in Sudan who has a starving four-year-old child flourish as a human being? Although this seems like an extreme situation, a significant percentage of the global population lives under conditions of privation, harm, and mistreatment. For several billion people on this planet, my friend's question isn't hypothetical. While everyone has the capacity to flourish and can, even under the worst conditions, flourish to some extent, no one facing desperate material and political conditions can be said to be flourishing in any meaningful sense.

In economically developed societies, many of us currently live in relative comfort and have the basic material necessities of life, although an increasingly significant number of people face poverty and homelessness since the neoliberal capitalist economy prioritizes corporate profits over human needs. Nonetheless, even those who are better off today live with a pervasive sense of social insecurity and uncertainty which limits our ability to flourish. We might have a good job and a decent standard of living one day, and lose them the next. In this sense we are socially insecure. Moreover, we live in deeply polarized societies; cultural and political conflicts have become so intense that they are undermining our democratic institutions – as limited as they are. This toxic political environment also militates against a flourishing life. Whether we are experiencing extreme poverty and privation, or living in relatively comfortable conditions, we must still acknowledge the impact of external conditions on our

Chapter 7: **Human Flourishing**

opportunities to live a flourishing life.

Internal and external conditions meld in our lives, but the conceptual distinction helps us to separate the forces that are impinging on us at any one time. We need to see them as interconnected, mutually conditioned aspects of our lives. External conditions profoundly affect internal conditions and vice versa. Thus, to flourish in this world, we need to develop simultaneously internal and external conditions which support and sustain each other in a synergistic way as part of creating a good and meaningful life.

For example, to the extent that we can transform ourselves through meditative practices, we can be more effective in our political practice and can further develop our sensitivity and motivation to engage in activities whose goal is to alleviate human suffering and the suffering of other species. At the same time, our political practice should aim not at simply social transformation but at individual transformation also. With this understanding, mindfulness practice is itself a component of political praxis and political praxis becomes a component of mindfulness.

Creating a flourishing life requires us to cultivate internal conditions for real happiness while transforming external conditions so that they reinforce the internal ones and provide the material, cultural, and political supports for a dignified, meaningful, and happy life. To achieve this, we need to make transformative changes at both the individual and societal levels. The personal and the political spheres of life are mutually related and equally important to the process of transformation.

Dimensions of human flourishing

Recognizing that the internal and external conditions for flourishing can never be attained in some complete or perfect form, that flourishing is a lifelong process, I offer below an outline of the salient dimensions of human flourishing. I'll bring together the perspectives of Aristotle, Gotama, Marx, and Nussbaum to identify a broad range of human capacities which contribute to a flourishing life. The point of this outline is not to establish a to-do list of activities that one needs to accomplish in order to be happy. Nor is it a prescription for getting the most out of life by actualizing as many dimensions as is possible. Rather, the list helps us settle our own priorities in terms of our finitude – our finite life span and limited opportunities. My outline aims to capture the richness and complexity of human flourishing, and the kind of institutional supports that are needed to ensure that all human beings have the opportunity to flourish.

Physical/sensual dimension

According to a widespread trope in conventional Buddhism, physical and sensuous contact with the world gives rise to suffering because it leads to clinging and attachment. Buddhism's penchant for renunciation aims to take us away from sensuous existence and toward nirvanic states in which we are free from attachments. By and large secular Buddhists reject this notion of renunciation and believe that a basic dimension of human flourishing is fully experiencing the full range of emotional and sensuous contact with each other and the world. Instead, they seek to realize the body's potential for a robust engagement in the world, thus making the body as strong and healthy as it can be under the circumstances, both internally and externally. We should fully occupy our bodies so as to experience sensations mindfully in the present, often in the context of significant relationships.

Intellectual/cognitive dimension

As we've seen, Aristotle saw rationality as the feature that distinguishes human beings from other animals. While recent research has revealed that animals have more cognitive capacities than Aristotle recognized, the human capacity for abstract thought and creativity is qualitatively different. Actualizing our unique cognitive capacities to the fullest extent thus constitutes a dimension of human flourishing. We develop this capacity to understand ourselves, others, and the world in part through our natural curiosity, but primarily to solve problems in our personal interactions, social life, and material existence. Our cognitive capacities enable us to discover new ways of understanding the world and our place in the universe. In combination with our emotions and intuition, our cognitive capacities also enable us to imagine and create works of art and culture which have a profound impact on us and contribute to our spiritual lives.

Imagination/play dimension

It isn't necessary to be a child to understand that one of the most rewarding and meaningful dimensions of life is play – spontaneous, voluntary, pleasurable and flexible activity performed for the sake of the enjoyment of an individual or a group. There is an old English proverb which expresses the value of play in a well-rounded life: 'All work and no play makes Jack a dull boy'. We could also say that without play, our life rarely flourishes.

Productive, social labor dimension

For Marx, this was the defining human capacity, essential to a flourishing life. In a capitalist society, labor is alienating, exploitative, and oppressive; as a result, we are degraded and our humanity is stunted in thrall to maximizing the financial gains of a tiny minority. In a democratic socialist society, we'd have the resources and institutional support to wield our mental, physical, and emotional capacities, to work together with others in creating goods and services which meet everybody's needs. Through productive social labor, we develop our capacity for autonomy and creativity in workplace settings. And by participating in democratic workplace structures to determine production processes, materials, and goals, we express our capacity for self-governance, teamwork, and sensitivity to nature.

Emotional intimacy/interconnection dimension

Nussbaum has rightly emphasized that our natural tendencies toward sociality, cooperation, and love go to the heart of human flourishing. We are social animals who need to have strong interpersonal connections with others to have a meaningful life. Numerous studies, including a recent meta-review by Naito et al,[124] have shown that a lack of such connections leads not just to a less flourishing life, but to a shorter one. We need to develop our capacity for emotional intimacy to relate to others kindly, to develop deep relationships of love and support with family members and close friends. At the same time, as Buddhists emphasize, we need to recognize the inevitable pain of loss and disappointment that accompany all human relationships.

Participation in social groups dimension

Sociality finds expression in work, education, community, and political activity. We spend much of our time in groups. Many people find group interactions fraught and painful, yet we can't avoid them. So, we need to make an effort to work with others skillfully so we can enjoy contributing to groups in a fruitful way. Flourishing in group work starts with recognizing others, and in turn being recognized by them, as valuable colleagues entitled to respect and dignity. We can find support and protection through group participation.

Political involvement and activism dimension

For Aristotle, Marx, and Nussbaum, participation as citizens in political and civic affairs contributes to a flourishing life. Each of course has a unique perspective on the nature of politics and the role of citizens. All would agree that actualizing our capacity to take part in democratic decision-making processes is an essential element of a flourishing life. Marx saw this human capacity as the life blood of the democratic movement to overcome oppressive and exploitative social structures.

Meaning/spiritual dimension

John Hick argued that all religions, including conventional Buddhism, proclaim the human need and capacity to engage with a feature of life 'which involves reference beyond the natural world to God or gods or to the Absolute or to a transcendent order or process'.[125] As a secular Buddhist, I am not religious in that sense. But the lack of belief in a transcendent dimension does not mean that a spiritual dimension is irrelevant. Far from it. When we seek our most important goals and commitments in this finite life, and identify our ultimate values, we are engaging with the spiritual dimension. This, too, is an important aspect of a flourishing life. In his book *This Life*, Martin Hägglund dubs this inquiry our 'spiritual freedom' – our ability to find the purpose of our life through normative inquiry, rather than one prescribed by natural instincts.[126]

Experience of 'oneness' or the non-dual dimension

Many conventional Buddhists hold that the cultivation of a non-dual perspective – one that overcomes our habitual perceptions of dualities in our experience, including selfhood – must underpin our efforts to attain nirvana. However, we don't need to accept the traditional Buddhist notions of nirvana or not-self to relish our occasional experiences of a seamless oneness in our existence. To flourish in life, we must develop the capacity to be present in the world in a full way, without ego involvement, and to experience the wonder and mystery of life – what Stephen Batchelor calls 'the everyday sublime'.

Relationship to nature dimension

Realizing oneness sets us up to experience interconnectedness with nature. We come to appreciate our place in the biosphere and among all forms of life that we live with. We can't flourish without care and respect for all that lives. We must reject the notion of human beings as masters and dominators of our eco-system. To flourish as human beings, we must seek to reduce the suffering of all sentient beings.

Why not the flourishing of all beings?

The last dimension in my proposed outline leads to an important objection raised about the notion of *human* flourishing. Why nominate it as the ultimate goal of a secular, radically engaged approach? Isn't this, as Peter Singer and others have argued, a form of speciesism which sees other sentient beings as merely instrumental to the human pursuit of a good, meaningful, and happy life?[127] Shouldn't we move away from this perspective and adopt the view that all sentient beings (and perhaps the ecosystem) deserve to be equally valued?

These crucial questions have evoked vigorous debate. While I recognize the important points made by those who critique speciesism and their well-intentioned efforts to expand ethical behavior to a wider circle of beings, the goal of human flourishing remains important and valid. In the first place, as noted above, treating other life forms and the natural world with respect and compassion is a criterion for human flourishing. At a minimum, in our path of human flourishing, we need to do as little harm as possible to other sentient beings. A meaningful, flourishing life includes a deep sense of connection with, and care for, the natural world.

My other reason for focusing on specifically human flourishing stems from our uncertainty about what flourishing means for other life forms, or even whether this concept makes sense in this context. We certainly know when we cause other beings to suffer in many situations, such as when we inflict pain and suffering on animals in our industrial-agricultural complex, or when we destroy the environment in the pursuit of maximising profit. We can discern when and why our companion animals are happier or more satisfied. (I definitely know when our dog is in a good and playful mood.) But I think we exaggerate our level of understanding when we claim to know what a flourishing life is for a giraffe or a red robin. So, rather than apply the notion of flourishing to all beings, it is wiser in my view to restrict the discussion of flourishing to human life.

A lifelong process

In proposing a comprehensive notion of human flourishing, I am not setting up an alternative ultimate goal as a secular substitute to the notion of nirvana as the complete and permanent release from suffering. Human flourishing does not lead to any final, perfect end of that kind. Rather, it's a process in which each individual develops their human capacities for a good life in ways that are most valuable to them while contributing to the flourishing of others and the wellbeing of other life forms. By integrating the Buddhist emphasis on

Chapter 7: **Human Flourishing**

cultivating the internal conditions for flourishing with Nussbaum's and Marx's insights about the necessary external conditions, we can begin to construct a practical theory of human flourishing that addresses a comprehensive set of human capacities, as well as the integral connection between individual flourishing and a just society.

Chapter 8
The Five Core Life Tasks

Buddhism has many lists which summarize its doctrines and key concepts, some of which you have encountered in earlier chapters where I've critically analyzed such core teachings and insights as the Four Noble Truths, the eightfold path, and the three marks of existence. You can even find 'lists of lists' in books about Buddhism, including in Buswell and Lopez's *The Princeton Dictionary of Buddhism*, which has 37 pages of lists, beginning with 'one vehicle' and ending with the 'one hundred dharmas of the Yogacara school'.[128] Gotama taught in a preliterate society, and couched much of his teaching in the form of lists of points that his followers could use as they recalled what he'd said. Having succinct lists to summarize key notions and practices is helpful for those who are trying to memorize the teachings in their original form and for those who are learning about them for the first time. However, literacy and modern forms of communication diminish the usefulness of storing and communicating ideas in this way.

While I initially found the lists helpful as a pedagogical device, I've never seen them as the necessary starting point for my effort to meld Gotama's insights with radical political perspectives. For example, why must we stick to the original formula of an eightfold path in seeking to define a flourishing life? We might incorporate some of its folds but add others that aren't part of the Buddhist canon. Or we might group the folds into different categories than the tripartite division of wisdom, ethics, and meditation.

In this regard, I depart somewhat from Stephen Batchelor's approach while retaining his focus on the link between core life tasks and human flourishing. I am indebted to Batchelor for developing a secular approach to the dharma. As I noted in the Preface, he provided my entry into Buddhism and I have continued to learn much from him as he continues to develop his perspective. However, while he has presented a new take on the dharma – 'Buddhism 2.0' as he calls it – he argues that his work '…needs to be founded upon canonical source texts, be able to offer a coherent interpretation of key practices, doctrines, and ethical precepts, and to provide a sufficiently rich and integrated theoretical model of the dharma to serve as the basis for a flourishing of human existence'.[129]

As someone who trained as a Buddhist monk for many years and has engaged in a deep study of Buddhist texts from a range of lineages, it makes sense that Batchelor would continue to have as his primary reference point the canonical source texts. He has creatively developed coherent interpretations of these texts which highlight the pragmatic and ethical aspects of Gotama's teachings. However, I take a different view of the canonical texts. Buddhist insights, interpreted to meet our contemporary challenges as Batchelor renders them, offer us valuable insights on the human condition and how to live a more fulfilling life. In this way they furnish a crucial starting point for developing a comprehensive theory and practice of individual and social transformation. Yet, for me, they are not *the* starting point but one of several essential perspectives. I encountered Buddhism long after I had already engaged in a lifelong period of study and activism based on radical political perspectives, while also being strongly influenced by feminism, psychological theories, my own experience with insight-oriented forms of psychological therapy, and pragmatist philosophies. The challenge for me has been to integrate Gotama's teachings with these other perspectives.

So, when Katya de Kadt, Karsten Struhl, and I decided to write an article about the core life tasks for a secular, radically engaged Buddhist – someone who believes in the need for the simultaneous cultivation of the Buddhist virtues of mindfulness and compassion, as well as the radical transformation of exploitative and oppressive social institutions – we didn't adhere strictly to either the Four Noble Truths or Stephen Batchelor's reinterpretation of the Four Noble Truths as four tasks. While we found Batchelor's notion of four tasks to be the preferable starting point, and the five tasks that we proposed overlap to some extent with Batchelor's tasks, we revised and moved beyond them in important respects.[130] In this chapter, I delineate and further explore the core life tasks for secular Buddhists who believe in radical social transformation.

The Four Noble Truths and Batchelor's four tasks

To understand the ways in which the core life tasks of a secular, radically engaged Buddhist both revise and move beyond Batchelor's four tasks, it will be helpful to recap the Four Noble Truths and Batchelor's four tasks.

As I discussed in Chapters 1 and 2, the Four Noble Truths represent a conventional statement of the Buddhist view of suffering, its causes and remedy. The first truth is that life always involves suffering, in both obvious and subtle ways. Even at our happiest moments, an undercurrent of anxiety and unsatisfactoriness always exists. Why? The second truth is that the cause of this suffering is the natural tendency to crave or desire pleasant experiences and to push away or take an aversive stance to experiences which are unpleasant. This tendency to be reactive (desire the pleasant, push away the unpleasant) is in turn based on a fundamental ignorance of ourselves and reality; namely, our delusory belief in a separate, substantial self – an 'I' or 'me' – that has control and complete autonomy. As a result, we fail to recognize that we are inextricably connected to the web of constantly changing causes and conditions which constitute reality. Clinging and the illusion of the self inevitably lead us to relate to our experiences in ways which not only cause us to harm ourselves and suffer but cause harm and suffering to others.

However, according to the third truth, we can cease clinging and understand the true nature of ourselves and the world, thus putting an end to suffering. The fourth truth reveals how we can achieve this result, by following the eightfold path – living ethically, practicing meditation, and developing wisdom (including understanding the Four Noble Truths). Through the cultivation of these three aspects of the eightfold path, we can gain freedom from suffering just as the Buddha did.

Batchelor's secular reinterpretation highlights the to-do message of this teaching, and brings forward the four interrelated tasks in it to transform our lives and promote human flourishing in this world. These tasks thus replace the conventional four ultimate 'truths' or articles of faith. In Batchelor's account each 'truth' morphs into an injunction or 'task'. Read as a series, they create the pithy acronym 'ELSA':

1) **E**mbrace life;
2) **L**et reactivity be;
3) **S**ee reactivity stop;
4) **A**ctualize a path.

Instead of the truth claim that life necessarily involves suffering, Batchelor's first task enjoins us to embrace life in all its complexity, including suffering. While the second truth locates the cause of suffering in our clinging and false sense of the self, his second task is to recognize and 'let be' our reactivity to pleasant and unpleasant experiences, which causes harm to ourselves and others. He reconfigures the third truth – we can end suffering by ceasing to cling and holding to a false view of the self – as the task of savoring the experience of a mind free of reactivity – its spaciousness, calm and clarity (which satisfies the definition of nirvana in the Pali Canon).

For the fourth task – actualizing the path – he retains the notion of a path consisting of eight undertakings which, when put into practice, promote our own and other beings' flourishing in this life, rather than individual transcendence to eternal nirvana.

Batchelor's four tasks differ from the Four Noble Truths in several other important respects:

Chapter 8: **The Five Core Life Tasks**

- ☆ He doesn't highlight suffering as the salient experience of life, but places suffering in the context of our whole life experience. The task is to recognize and embrace 'the whole catastrophe' so that we can move toward more ethical and fulfilling ways of living.
- ☆ The cause of suffering in the second truth is rooted in an *internal* problem; we naturally cling and harbor a deluded view of self. As I understand Batchelor's current perspective, he sees reactivity as having multiple sources: 1) the existential dimension of the human organism and its environment, 2) the psychological dimension based in family relationships, and 3) the social dimension based on forms of Othering, exploitation, and discrimination.
- ☆ The third truth is based on the goal of the complete and permanent extinction of suffering by eliminating craving and delusion. In the four-task approach, however, the goal is to create a space of non-reactivity in which we're free to respond more ethically and creatively to life's varied and changing situations.
- ☆ The eightfold path in Batchelor's approach focuses on improving our lives in this life by cultivating a balance of virtues and skills and opening up access to non-reactive experience. In recent years, as reported on the Secular Buddhist Network website,[131] Batchelor has not only presented the path factors in a different order than in the standard account but also offered a new interpretation of each path factor's role in the path, based on the original Pali terms in the canon. This reconfiguration emphasizes the connection between the path factors and human flourishing. In his reconfiguration, Batchelor has two categories of tasks: internal/contemplative, and external/active ones. The latter are just as important as the former. In this way, his notion of the path is more socially oriented. The goal of individual salvation and complete freedom from suffering gives way to an ambition to live a flourishing life which contributes to a wider culture of awakening.

In discussing the core life tasks of a secular, radically engaged Buddhist, I will follow Batchelor in insisting that the tasks are essentially pragmatic and ethical. They serve human flourishing in this life, rather than the attainment of other-worldly nirvanic peace and liberation. But I add an explicitly political, activist dimension which, up till now, has been implicit in Batchelor's approach but not fully developed.

I acknowledge that, for some socially engaged Buddhists, revising and going beyond the Four Noble Truths might seem presumptuous and disrespectful toward existing varieties of Buddhism, including Stephen Batchelor's secular revision of the dharma. I don't offer my approach as the 'right way' or the 'true' form of socially engaged Buddhism. Instead, based on my interests and values as a secular, radically engaged Buddhist, I'm attempting to lay out the essential elements of a spiritual, psychological, and political path aimed not just at the reduction of the suffering of individuals but also at dismantling the social, political, and economic systems which cause harm and suffering to all beings. I offer this contribution in the hope that Buddhist practitioners, especially those who understand the need for being active in resolving social problems, will consider joining a larger movement for radical social transformation.

Five core tasks for secular, radically engaged Buddhists

These tasks are based on certain beliefs about human capacities (for good and bad), the causes of suffering, and the need to integrate individual transformation with radical social change. While the tasks retain some of the key ideas from mainstream Buddhism and use Batchelor's notion of tasks, they incorporate a broader range of human activities, including an explicitly political dimension.

#1

Recognize, accept, and embrace our finite life in all its complexity

In the 1960s, there was a very small Left political group in the United States

Chapter 8: **The Five Core Life Tasks**

that existed for just a short time but seriously engaged with the first task in a political context. The group was the product of numerous faction fights and splits within a weakened US Left. Its name and intent, was taken from a book written in 1958 by C.L.R. James and Grace C. Lee, in collaboration with Cornelius Castoriadis – *Facing Reality*.[132] Although the Facing Reality group never had much influence beyond a small circle of people, the group was notable for its effort to examine the complex and difficult situation that Leftists faced in the USA in new ways; Facing Reality rejected the various Left political orthodoxies of the time and advocated for workers' self-emancipation.

One of the hardest things for all of us to do is to face our situation in all its complexity, changes, and challenges. Yet that is the first task we need to engage with. For mainstream Buddhists, the first of the Four Noble Truths holds that suffering is an inevitable part of any human life. Acknowledging it allows us to begin the process that leads to a nirvanic release from suffering.

From a secular, radically engaged perspective, two problems arise out of this mainstream Buddhist belief. First, a complete release from suffering seems implausible. Second, suffering is just one experience among many in someone's complex life process.

Our initial task is to face our multilayered experience just as it is, including its tragic dimension. We will all experience the '10,000 joys and 10,000 sorrows' of a human life. While we have some ability to shape the course of our life in order to reduce suffering and experience more joy and happiness, much of what we experience is beyond our control. A life without suffering would not be a human life.

To come to terms with the human condition we need to move away from an ego-centered perspective in which 'I' stand alone as a separate being, striving to fulfill 'my' needs and wants by controlling what happens in my world. The first step in creating an ethical, flourishing, and activist life consists in recognizing that we are not isolated, separate individuals, and that we have limited control over what we experience because we're just a small part of a web of changing causes and conditions. It's not enough to grasp these truths conceptually – we need to feel them in our hearts and bones. Facing reality in this manner is not a process of gaining some detached perspective from 'above' the world but being both clear-eyed and passionately connected to our life experience.

When we face our own personal joys and sorrows of our own life in this way, we can resonate with the joys and sorrows in the lives of others, both near and far. Thich Nhat Hanh calls this sensibility interbeing: we are inextricably connected to and interdependent with other beings and nature.[133] So, we can't just focus on our own needs; we must respond to the suffering of others in different social locations, statuses, and conditions from our own.

#2
Understand the three basic causes of suffering
The second task for a secular, radically engaged Buddhist is to recognize what causes our suffering and limits our flourishing in this world. Here, too, the task goes beyond attaining a correct understanding of our situation; an embodied mindful response to the actual experience of suffering must anchor our conceptual clarity.

For mainstream Buddhists, the second of the Four Noble Truths is that the cause of suffering resides in each individual's craving for good or pleasant experiences, and aversion to bad or painful experiences. Suffering thus arises from the unskillful thoughts, speech, and actions which arise from craving. This doctrine resembles the Christian one of 'original sin' in suggesting that human beings are selfish creatures – an assumption that also underpins rightwing economic and political theories.

From a secular, radically engaged perspective, the mainstream Buddhist view of suffering is too limited and fails to recognize that suffering has multiple causes. As I noted, Batchelor has asserted that our reactivity which causes suffering has three sources: our instinctual reactions to unpleasant or frightening experiences; our psychological history and development, which often includes some measure of trauma; and the social institutions and cultural influences which contribute to reactivity and suffering, including racism.

Chapter 8: **The Five Core Life Tasks**

While agreeing that suffering has multiple sources, I suggest we categorize them somewhat differently. My three sources of suffering are: the fact that we are finite, limited beings in a perilous world; how we typically relate to our own experiences; and social systems which cause harm. On this view, the second task becomes to probe, both cognitively and experientially, these three interrelated causes of the '10,000 sorrows' of life. The sources of our suffering are:

- ☆ The *inevitable pains and losses connected with our finite life* and our relative lack of control over the processes of sickness, aging, death, loss, not getting what we want, and getting what we don't want. This list coincides with Gotama's in his first discourse, where he defined suffering (dukkha) in these terms. But some Buddhists view these inevitable pains of life as distinct from suffering per se, which springs from our relating unskillfully to our experiences, both good and bad. I think it is more useful to view this aspect of our lives as a separate form of suffering.
- ☆ Our biologically evolved tendency to cling or relate to what we experience in a reactive way, based on wanting something (greed), or wanting to avoid something (aversion, hatred), as well as our fundamental tendency to view ourselves and the world from the deluded perspective of the isolated, egoistical self. *The tendency to cling and a delusory understanding of the self* together combine to create suffering beyond the inevitable suffering we experience as finite, limited beings. This is the notion of suffering which the second of the Four Noble Truths highlights.
- ☆ *Social systems of exploitation and oppression* (capitalism, racism, sexism, homophobia, ageism, disrespect of persons with disabilities, and so on) mutually interact with and reinforce our tendencies to crave and to cling and have a delusory understanding of the self. In addition, these structures of exploitation and oppression directly harm

individuals and groups in various ways, including through material privation, social insecurity, and a sense of social isolation, while reinforcing the harmful human tendencies that develop out of the three poisons of greed, hatred, and delusion.

We need to discern how these sources of suffering interact with and fortify each other. For example, as an exploitative socio-economic system, capitalism reinforces our craving for and clinging to material/consumer objects and facilitates destructive forms of human interaction based on pervasive competition, domination, and deliberately engineered social insecurity. At the same time, our tendency to crave and cling supports policies and social institutions that generate domination and subordination, exploitation, and oppression. Each of the sources of suffering contributes to an interrelated set of causes and conditions which cause suffering.

One way of portraying the mutual interaction of these sources of suffering is in the figure below:

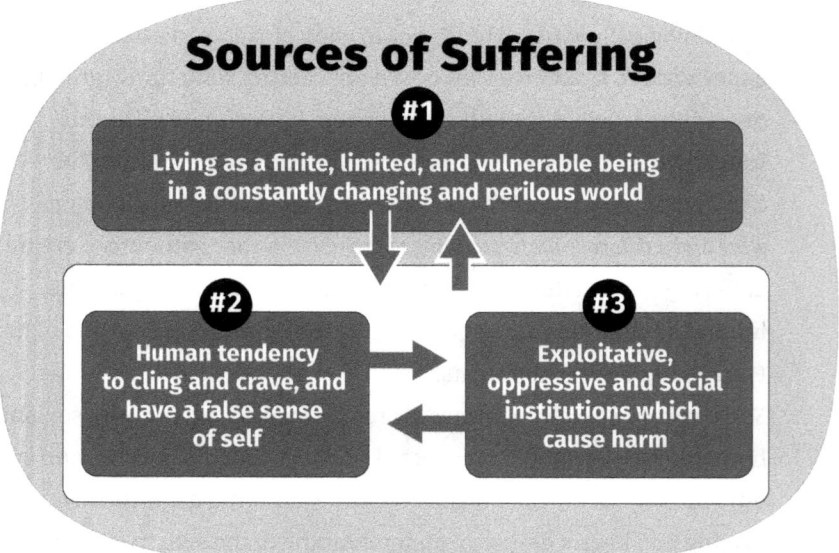

Chapter 8: **The Five Core Life Tasks**

The individual and social sources of suffering thus mutually interact and interpenetrate. Both kinds of mainsprings of suffering permeate a world in which we are limited, vulnerable beings, subject to the vagaries of a constantly changing set of causes and conditions.

The point of the second task is to confront these sources in a wise, mindful, and compassionate way, so we can reduce suffering and contribute to the flourishing of all. The well-known Serenity Prayer, attributed to the theologian Reinhold Niebuhr, pinpoints the need for practical wisdom in working with our difficulties: 'God grant me the serenity to accept the things I cannot change; Courage to change the things I can; And wisdom to know the difference.' In a similar way, understanding the three sources of suffering provides us with an important framework for responding appropriately to life's challenges:

☆ Recognition of our human vulnerability in the context of the inevitable anguish we experience in even the most fortunate life enables us to accept and embrace those aspects of life which cannot be changed. We don't blame ourselves or others for the conditions that cannot be changed and that we all must face. Instead, the appropriate response is to feel compassion for ourselves and others. We can develop a sense of serenity and equanimity in response to these experiences. And finally, we can recognize that being mindfully present with sickness, aging, death, and the loss of those we love can be the occasion for maturation and personal growth. This is a point that Winton Higgins has made in retrieving Freud's psychoanalytic insight that we need to work through the mourning process if we wish to be able to flourish after a major loss. Mourning exemplifies the dharmic task of embracing our moments of intense suffering. To accept life in this way, we must 'learn to ride the tiger of impermanence.'[134]

☆ Awareness of our tendency to cling and hold to a delusory sense of the self can provide us with a realistic sense of who we really are as human beings, and how to temper our reactivity. In response to our own reactivity, we can become more mindful and fully present by recognizing when we are being reactive and causing harm to ourselves and others. We can bring compassion and love to reactivity, turning the energies of greed, hatred, and delusion toward good will, non-harming, and wisdom. To the extent that we exercise agency over our emotions, thoughts, and actions, we can transform ourselves.

☆ Recognition of the social sources of suffering enables us to see how suffering occurs in a social context. To reduce suffering and promote flourishing, we need not only to cultivate certain skills and virtues as part of a path of personal transformation based on meditation and other practices. We also have to transform the very social institutions which cause harm and prevent us from flourishing. We must work toward personal and social transformation at the same time.

To paraphrase Niebuhr, distinguishing between different sources of suffering and seeing how they interact provides us with the wisdom to relate appropriately to challenges, and thus to act and speak in ways which reduce suffering and promote flourishing.

#3
Use our capacities for wisdom, mindfulness, and compassion to reduce suffering and promote flourishing
Awareness of the three sources of suffering equips us to discern the situations in which we can make positive changes in our lives while staying within the limits of our agency. We need to stay alert to how and when we react and, as Batchelor says, to 'let reactivity be'. But mindfulness of our reactivity is not the end of the process. The third task is to use our mindfulness, compassion, and wisdom to inform our actions and words directed at reducing suffering and promoting flourishing for all. In short, it is to act and speak ethically.

This task contrasts with the approach in the third of the Four Noble

Chapter 8: **The Five Core Life Tasks**

Truths, which promises personal salvation from all suffering in a permanent state of nirvana. When we attain nirvana, we have left the human world of conditionality. Such a drastic leap of faith into a post-human condition awakens deep skepticism in the secular mind.

Embedded in the natural world as we are, we cannot achieve the complete and permanent cessation of craving and clinging. As I noted in Chapter 2, the task is not to eliminate greed, hatred, and delusion but to shift the balance away from these three poisons and toward mindfulness, compassion, and wisdom. By establishing a different relationship between unskillful and skillful qualities of the mind, we can reduce suffering, but not leave it behind altogether.

Shifting the balance in this way is not solely or even primarily a personal matter – one intended to provide an individual with a happier, less stressful life. And the process of shifting the balance occurs not just through solitary meditative practices. As long as other people are suffering from individual and social harm, we cannot be totally at peace or liberated. As long as social institutions reinforce greed, hatred, and delusion, we cannot flourish individually or as a society. We need to engage in collective forms of struggle which challenge systemic sources of suffering. We cultivate mindfulness, compassion, and wisdom in political activism as well as in meditation.

Finally, while human flourishing constitutes the highest good for secular, radically engaged Buddhists, we can only achieve it if we value other forms of life and the natural world. We are embedded in the web of life. An appreciation of our connection with the ecosystem and an understanding that all sentient beings experience suffering requires us to relate to the non-human world with care and compassion, to be guided by the principle of non-harming. We cannot flourish if we see other species and the ecosystem reduced to objects to satisfy our own convenience and satisfaction. From our interactions at a micro level to global humanity's macro structures, we need to act with a sense of care for the non-human world.

#4
Engage in a life-long path of transformation based on skillful virtues, wisdom, meditative practices, an ethical life, and political activism

This core life task of a secular radically engaged Buddhist comes close to the Buddhist eightfold path in promoting the need to cultivate a range of capacities that underpin a meaningful and ethical life. These capacities encompass cognition, affective states, and bodily sensations; intentions and actions; and personal and communal practices. But while this life task includes certain elements of the eightfold path, the range of capacities is expanded to include an understanding of critical social theories and political activism.

To contribute to the reduction of suffering and to the promotion of human flourishing through individual transformation and collective action, we must commit ourselves to an integrated path based on:

- ☆ **Skillful virtues and attitudes.** While I mostly shy away from Buddhist lists, two of them do identify virtues and attitudes that we need to cultivate. One list is the 'four immeasurables' or brahmaviharas, which I discussed in relation to meditation practice in Chapter 4: the four emotional tones of loving kindness, compassion, sympathetic joy, and equanimity. Another essential set of virtues and attitudes appears in the list of 'six perfections' or *paramitas*: generosity, non-harming, patience, effort, concentration, and wisdom. The development of these virtues counters our tendency toward self-interest and egotism while encouraging us to enact our interconnection with others. They provide the basis for peaceful, cooperative, and egalitarian relationships and guide us in developing a society which promotes human flourishing, the welfare of other creatures, and a sustainable relation to the ecosystems that we are part of.
- ☆ **Wisdom.** As Batchelor has pointed out, the coming of wisdom

Chapter 8: **The Five Core Life Tasks**

requires us to develop a sense of curiosity, open-mindedness, and healthy skepticism which saves us from becoming too attached to particular perspectives, and viewing situations in black or white terms through the use of dualistic categories. Having an open and receptive attitude toward knowledge is a precondition for cultivating wisdom regarding the following essential components of human understanding:

- The three basic aspects of human experience: impermanence, interconnectedness, and the sources of our '10,000 sorrows';
- the conditioned nature of all events and processes as well as our capacity to effect change within that context;
- the essential aspects of the human condition as biologically evolved, psychologically shaped, and socially mediated; and
- the history and processes of socio-economic systems and their relationship to human beings and nature.

☆ **Meditative practices.** As discussed in Chapter 4, meditation helps us to reduce clinging and reactivity, enables us to develop a critical and comprehensive understanding of the human condition, promotes ethical behavior, and facilitates skillful engagement in movements for social change.

☆ **Ethics.** This area of cultivation promotes the values of care, compassion, non-harm, and a respect for the interconnection of all sentient and living beings. Rather than rigidly prescribing and prohibiting actions in a set of rules, this ethical approach empowers us to make choices in each unique situation based on the values listed above. However, as Batchelor has noted, we often face situations in which the appropriate ethical response is not clear; we face uncertainty 'not only because we can never gain full knowledge of all the factors in a situation, but also because we can't predict the results of our actions. Even with the best of intentions, what we do may not lead to positive results.[135] For this reason, the cultivation of ethics depends on mindfulness won through meditation and everyday experience.

☆ **Social Engagement and Political Activism.** Active participation with others in groups and political movements in our community rounds out a life path oriented toward flourishing. As I have argued throughout, social and systemic sources of suffering stand in the way of a flourishing life for all. However, like every other aspect of the path, the commitment to social engagement and political activism depends on the cultivation of the other life tasks mentioned. We are not born as mindful and compassionate activists. We develop that capacity as part of an integrated path oriented toward flourishing.

#5
Make transformative changes at both the individual and societal levels

There is no comparable Noble Truth to the fifth task, which is to integrate transformative changes at both the individual and social levels to reduce suffering and promote flourishing. The traditional Four Noble Truths do not make that connection between the individual and society because the cause of and remedy for suffering is primarily located in the individual. As Batchelor has elaborated the four tasks, the path does entail a social dimension; and the rationale of the path is both individual and social transformation. However, Batchelor's notion of social transformation in the form of a community of awakening is not well developed and the need for collective political activism is not discussed. On the other hand, in his book, *This Life: Secular Faith and Spiritual Freedom*, Martin Hägglund does make an explicit link between an individual's cultivation of spiritual freedom and the goal of creating a democratic socialist society which 'seeks to provide the institutional, political, and material conditions for spiritual freedom.'[136] His concept of spiritual freedom approximates to human flourishing.

Whether we call our vision spiritual freedom or human flourishing, it

Chapter 8: The Five Core Life Tasks

requires progress towards a democratic, ecosocialist, anti-racist, and anti-patriarchal society. To achieve this, we need to make transformative changes at both the individual and societal levels. The personal and the political spheres of life are mutually related and equally important to the process of transformation.

For example, to the extent that we can transform ourselves through meditative practices, we become more effective in our political practice. At the same time, our political activism should aim not just at social transformation but at individual transformation. From this perspective, mindfulness practice serves fruitful political activism, and political activism offers an arena in which mindfulness and compassion can develop as we work with others to achieve our political goals.

There is no magic formula for *how* to integrate individual and social transformation in our everyday lives. How should we balance meditative practices with engagement in political activity in terms of time and commitment? How do we assess whether we need to focus more on one or the other? When we are in the midst of a political crisis requiring intense involvement, how do we maintain our ability to cultivate mindfulness in formal practice? How do we practice self-care while not pushing aside the political commitments that we have made?

These questions don't have easy answers. Like difficult moral situations, we need to bring to the fore a sense of open-mindedness, discernment, and equanimity to navigate these complex situations. While we may sometimes fail to identify the appropriate way of integrating individual and social transformation in our lives, we can reassess and choose a more balanced path. Facing the challenge to find the 'middle way' actually contributes to our flourishing.

I have laid out five core life tasks for a secular, radically engaged Buddhist: face our situation in all its complexity; understand the multiple sources of suffering; use our capacities for mindfulness and compassion to respond to suffering; cultivate a range of virtues, wise perspectives, ethical action, and mindful political action; and integrate individual and social transformation in our everyday lives.

I recognize that my discussion of these life tasks calls for further development in concrete situations we can find ourselves in. I don't see the list of core tasks that I've proposed as definitive or exhaustive. Others may nominate different crucial tasks or formulate the tasks in alternative ways. My hope is that my suggestions will stimulate reflection and discussion among Buddhists and political activists – a dialogue and inquiry into our most important commitments and tasks in this our one and only life.

Chapter 9
In a Nutshell

Well, my fellow activists: have I made a persuasive case that Buddhist insights and practices contribute to sustaining political activism, avoiding burnout, and creating a healthier internal life within progressive groups? Will you work with me to integrate these insights and practices into progressive political movements? And to my spiritual friends in Buddhist communities: do you think my arguments for a secular, radically engaged approach to Buddhism have merit? Will you join with me and others to challenge and transform the social sources of suffering while we continue to cultivate meditative and other skills and virtues to help us become more mindful and compassionate?

Those are the questions that matter most to me at the end of this inquiry. If this book has at least opened up a space for more discussion of these issues among activists and Buddhist communities, I will have accomplished my objective. My hope is that others will respond by offering their own perspectives and arguments. My own perspective stems from my life experiences, values, and interests, as well as the social location I inhabit. I am a white, middle class, and cisgender male who is a culturally Jewish agnostic and a radical political activist. Given the perspectival blinders and limits necessarily entailed in any particular social location, I know that those outside the location that I inhabit, particularly people of color, women, non-western people, and those in the LGBTQ community, will be able to offer valuable new insights and approaches on these issues. I welcome that.

In that spirit, I offer the following propositions for a secular, radically engaged approach as a way of summing up the arguments and perspectives presented in this book.

#1

The highest good of human life is to reduce suffering and promote human flourishing for all. Mainstream Buddhists identify the source of suffering as our tendency to react unmindfully to our experiences – craving the pleasant and pushing away the unpleasant – and to work from a false sense of the self as a separate, isolated entity. In contrast I suggest that there are three sources of suffering: our experience as finite, vulnerable beings in a perilous world; the human proclivity to lapse into greed, hatred, and delusion (the mainstream Buddhist view); and exploitative, oppressive, and discriminatory social systems which cause harm (the radical perspective). An adequate response to suffering needs to recognize the ways in which these three sources affect us and how they mutually interact to cause harm and suffering.

However, we shouldn't just aim to reduce suffering. We want all human beings to enjoy the preconditions for flourishing, to develop their capacities to have a meaningful, fulfilling, and ethical life. An adequate notion of human flourishing must include several perspectives and incorporate a wide range of human capacities and experiences. The first theorist to articulate the idea of flourishing, or eudaimonia, was Aristotle, who based his notion of human flourishing on our capacity for reason and living a virtuous life, including being temperate and courageous. Another crucial component of a theory of flourishing comes from Gotama, the historical Buddha. In response to our tendency to cause suffering through reactivity, he taught that we can cultivate certain skills and virtues through meditation, ethical action, and wisdom which enable us to reduce suffering and liberate ourselves to live a good life. But we also need to incorporate Marx's view of human nature, which highlights creative, productive labor as a central aspect of human flourishing; and Martha Nussbaum's capabilities approach, which specifies a set of conditions and capacities essential for a rich human life. Both Marx and Nussbaum identify the 'external' conditions for human flourishing. Bringing all these various perspectives together and by connecting the internal and external conditions for flourishing, we have the basis for developing an adequate notion of human flourishing.

#2

Gotama provided us with profound insights about how people tend to think, feel, and act in self-defeating ways which run counter to the cultivation of capacities essential to human flourishing. Not only do we tend to have a false understanding of our experiences, but our actions tend to be instinctively reactive, dominated by anger and/or greed, capacities which cause suffering to ourselves and others. But his approach to overcoming them calls for modification in several respects to satisfy modern conditions. The Buddhist prescription of renunciation and non-attachment as an antidote to craving has led to a tendency within Buddhism to deny the value of the body and sensuous experience. Gotama's teachings also lack a depth psychology which identifies how unconscious aspects of the mind play a key role in various forms of suffering. Finally, Gotama located suffering in the unskillful ways in which individuals relate to their experiences; today we need to factor in the social sources of suffering as a relatively autonomous source of suffering.

#3

Our capacities essential to human flourishing emerged and developed as part of our biological evolution and through cultural changes. They coexist with other human capacities, also biologically evolved and culturally developed, which cause suffering and unhappiness. All these capacities constitute our complex make-up. While secular, radically engaged Buddhists place a positive value on the capacities essential to human fulfillment and happiness, we don't believe that they constitute our 'true nature' or 'basic goodness', as some Buddhists assert. We are capable of a wide range of emotions, thoughts, and actions which are expressed in specific historical and social contexts.

#4

Since we are embedded in the natural world, we will always be subject to the causes and conditions of that world. Contrary to the perspective of many traditional forms of Buddhism, human flourishing is not achieved through transcendence to an end-state of unconditional liberation from suffering, nirvana. Instead of seeking transcendence from the conditioned world, our aspiration in this life should be to cultivate and develop the capacities that promote human flourishing while limiting the impact of capacities which cause suffering to ourselves and others. Our task is not to eliminate greed, hatred, and delusion, but to shift the balance away from these three tendencies and toward mindfulness, compassion, and wisdom.

#5

As Marx and others have stressed, social interaction engenders the capacities essential to human fulfillment. Even when we meditate alone, we are engaging in an ongoing internal dialogue dependent on previous social interactions. Meditation is a communal practice. Beginning with our earliest interactions with parents and other caretakers, and then in various social relationships, formal education processes, and the impact of such macro-social institutions as economic and political systems, our capacities for flourishing are either stunted or promoted to one degree or another.

#6

Given our inherently social nature and unique capacities, human flourishing must develop from the combined processes of individual and social transformation. The obstacles to flourishing spring from our proclivity to cause ourselves and others unnecessary suffering, as well as the ways in which social institutions directly harm people and incite greed and anger. A secular, radically engaged Buddhist understands that promoting human flourishing requires effort at both the individual level, such as meditative practices that reduce the role of reactivity and unskillful actions, and in political activism, which aims to transform the institutions in question.

#7

We thus need not only a psychology and phenomenology of suffering which Buddhism provides but also a philosophical and social perspective which grasps the complex interaction between the individual and society as a complement to Gotama's insights into individual experience. Such a perspective can be found in a non-deterministic, humanistic Marxism which helps us to understand the social causes and conditions that generate human suffering, as well as those that would enhance our potential for flourishing. When we bring together Buddhism and Marxism in dialogue, we gain the conceptual tools and practices to integrate individual and social transformation in our everyday lives.

#8

Western Buddhist practitioners mostly prioritize meditation as a spiritual path to a happier life. Although meditation does play a crucial role in reducing reactivity and facilitating mindful presence, the function and role of meditation in the west are problematic in three respects. First, meditation is typically viewed as an individual pursuit, a practice performed by a solitary individual primarily for the reduction of their own suffering and to have a happier private life. Second, instead of being seen as one of three complementary dimensions of the Buddhist path, along with wisdom and ethics, meditation has come to be seen as Buddhist practice as such. Thus, meditation and mindfulness practices are often marketed as disengaged from ethics and social engagement. Third, and as noted above, the ultimate goal of meditation for mainstream Buddhists is achieving individual access to a state of unconditional freedom and happiness – nirvana.

From the perspective of secular, radically engaged Buddhism, meditation not only enables us to develop the capacity for mindful presence that individuals need to flourish in this life, but helps us to become compassionate, discerning political activists committed to creating a society in which all human beings have the opportunity to flourish. Meditation is just one aspect of the nurturing of a broader set of skills, virtues, insights, and practices oriented toward the flourishing of all.

#9

The unfortunate emphasis on meditation as an individual practice divorced from ethical action and social engagement points to the need to prioritize the development of democratic communities of Buddhist practitioners. Such communities of 'spiritual friends' provide essential support for individuals to develop their own practice. In addition, they can play a crucial role in developing in sangha members the capacities and skills needed to contribute to a society in which the flourishing of each individual is mutually dependent on the flourishing of all. Such capacities include the ability to communicate mindfully and compassionately with others, to participate in discussions and make decisions democratically, and to foster broader forms of solidarity.

#10

Beyond the communities of Buddhist practitioners, we need to participate in political movements which contribute to a society which enables all human beings to flourish. We have a wide choice of movements to join, varying in terms of specific issues and approaches to social change. Whatever movements we do work within, we can't limit our objectives to simply ameliorating the key challenges that we face: socio-economic inequality, wars, the climate emergency, and other forms of human suffering. Unless we challenge and transform the root social sources of human suffering – neoliberal capitalism, patriarchy, racism, and so on – we will not be able create the conditions for a flourishing life for all.

Chapter 9: **In a Nutshell**

#11

Just as a non-dogmatic, humanistic Marxist perspective helps us to identify the shortcomings and problems in mainstream Buddhism, Buddhist insights and values illuminate some of the weaknesses in Left political movements. Although difficult economic and political conditions continue to obstruct the development of a powerful Left challenge to the status quo, internal problems have also hampered the Left. Left groups have nurtured an unhelpful model of political activism and a view of political correctness which have seriously weakened Left organizations.

The prevailing model of political activism – which I've dubbed homo radical politicus – rests on a narrow view of human capacities and is deeply gendered. It has facilitated the development of oppressive hierarchies and the mistreatment of activists within groups. At the same time, the widespread tendency for political groups to obsess about who has the 'correct line', has led to sectarian disputes and an overattachment to the outcomes of political action. Buddhism can play an important role in helping political movements avoid burn-out, organizational dysfunction, and debilitating internal disputes.

#12

A secular, radically engaged approach not only enables us to identify the shortcomings of mainstream Buddhism and Left politics but also to discern their valuable insights and practices essential to advancing human flourishing. Such an approach avoids binary ways of thinking (this view is right, that view is wrong) in favor of complexity and nuance. Viewing the 'truth' in all perspectives as provisional and subject to revision, we resist the tendency toward 'superiority conceit' that breeds a dismissive stance toward those who do not share our perspective. If we want to contribute to a movement toward human flourishing, then we must work with openness, an appreciation of diversity, and a willingness to cooperate with others in any way that furthers the cause.

The perspective in question emerges in a particular historical and social context. It is not a universal, timeless panacea. Rather, a secular and radically engaged Buddhist understands that our path will rely on a number of perspectives and practices in addition to Gotama's insights and Marx's radical social theory. We should be open to appreciating and incorporating any perspective and practice which contributes to the ultimate goal of flourishing for all.

A Note on Terminology

Throughout the book, I refer to the Buddha, which means the 'awakened one', as Gotama. In the ancient, northern Indian language of Pali, Gotama was the given name of the person who originated what we now know as Buddhism.

Pali is the canonical language of Theravada Buddhism, one of the early lineages of Buddhism. On the other hand, the canonical texts of Mahayana Buddhism, a later development, are in the Sanskrit language, although these texts were subsequently translated into Chinese, Tibetan, and other languages.

Following Stephen Batchelor and other secular Buddhists, I use the name Gotama to emphasize that the originator of what became Buddhism, an organized religion, was a human being, not a god-like figure as some ancestral Buddhists believe. From a secular Buddhist perspective, he was a human being who came to realize and teach a new way of living in the world which promotes human flourishing. While he was a great teacher and lived an exemplary ethical life, he did not have supernatural powers and didn't lay claim to any.

I also refer to some key Buddhist ideas and practices using the original Pali terms, often paired with English translations of them. For example, Gotama's focus was on recognizing the causes and remedy for suffering, or dukkha in Pali. As I discuss in the book, the Pali word dukkha stands for all the difficult and inevitable aspects of our lives: birth, aging, sickness, death, being separated from whom or what we love, being thrown together with whom or what we detest, not getting what we want, and our psycho-physical fragility.

Dukkha is one of the 'three marks of existence', an important Buddhist concept. The other two marks or characteristics of existence are impermanence (anicca in Pali) and not-self (anatta in Pali).

Finally, some Buddhist terms in Pali or Sanskrit are so well-known that no English translation is needed – for example, nirvana (Sanskrit) or nibbana (Pali). In the book I discuss the variety of meanings of this term within Buddhism.

Acknowledgements

This book is the fruit of many years of reflection, discussions, and activism in the political activist community and in Buddhist circles. There are too many people to list who in one way or another helped to shape the perspective presented in this book. However, I want to acknowledge those who had a direct role in this project.

First, a special thanks to Ramsey Margolis and Winton Higgins from The Tuwhiri Project. When I first suggested a book on the intersection of secular Buddhism and radical political activism, they were supportive and encouraging. Just as important, they helped me to clarify the purpose of the book and who I was trying to reach. Their guidance and prodding helped turn a disparate collection of essays and articles into a book with a coherent narrative.

Winton's editing of a series of drafts was extremely helpful, not only in terms of improving the content but in eliminating extraneous material. His exacting 'sentence re-engineering' made the book more concise and accessible. I am also deeply appreciative of Ramsey's copyediting skills and his commitment to high standards in book production.

As I noted in the book, Stephen Batchelor provided me, an agnostic radical political activist, with a path into Buddhism. Stephen's insightful writings on secular Buddhism have challenged me to rethink and examine my own views. He is a spiritual friend with whom I share the aspiration to make the secular dharma a crucial component of a culture of mindfulness and compassion. Even where my approach differs from his, I am deeply appreciative of his intellectual integrity and his ongoing effort to develop his perspective.

I want to thank Karsten Struhl and Katya de Kadt – my dharma buddies and comrades – for offering insightful suggestions for improving the book. We met just a few years ago and soon became close friends. Each of us had a long history in political activism, but then found that Buddhism offered essential insights and practices. I look forward to continuing to explore with Katya and Karsten a secular, radically engaged approach to Buddhism while we participate in movements which challenge social and systemic sources of suffering.

Several friends and family members read drafts of this book as it evolved. Thanks to Andy Feffer, Court Fisher, Keith Jackson, Ira Katz, George Knorr, Larry Lipschultz, Susan Slott Silver, and Sara Gia Trongone for their helpful comments and suggestions.

Finally, my thanks and love go to my wife and partner Sharon Tobias. Sharon is the first reader of what I write. While always supportive, she knows when I go off track or get lost in the weeds, and gently guides me back to the road ahead. In addition to her probing intelligence and editing skills, Sharon is an active participant and leader in the online groups affiliated with the Secular Buddhist Network, which has become a valuable place for secular Buddhists to connect online. Most important, my relationship with Sharon has enriched my life in so many ways; I can't imagine exploring my life's path without her.

References

Analayo, Bhikkhu (2021), *Superiority Conceit in Buddhist Traditions: A Historical Perspective* (Somerville, MA: Wisdom Publishing)

Aṅguttara Nikāya Worldly Conditions (AN 8.6). Accessed at https://suttacentral.net/an8.6/en/sujato?lang=en

Aristotle, Bartlett, R.C., & Collins, S.D. (2011), *Aristotle's Nicomachean Ethics* (Chicago: University of Chicago Press)

Batchelor, Martine and Batchelor, Stephen (2019), *What is this? Ancient questions for modern minds* (Wellington, New Zealand: Tuwhiri)

Batchelor, Stephen (1997), *Buddhism Without Beliefs* (New York: Riverhead Books)

Batchelor, Stephen (2010), *Confession of a Buddhist Atheist* (New York: Spiegel and Grau)

Batchelor, Stephen (2012), 'A Secular Buddhism', *Journal of Global Buddhism* vol.13, 87–107

Batchelor, Stephen (2015), *After Buddhism: Rethinking the Dharma for a Secular Age* (New Haven and London: Yale University Press)

Batchelor, Stephen (2017), *Secular Buddhism: Imagining the Dharma in an Uncertain World* (New Haven and London: Yale University Press)

Batchelor, Stephen, Feldman, Christina, and Weber, Akincano (2017), 'Understand, Realize, Give Up, Develop'. *Tricycle*. Accessed at https://tricycle.org/magazine/understand-realize-give-develop

Bhargava, Deepak and Luce, Stephanie (2023), *Practical Radicals: Seven Strategies to Change the World* (New York: New Press)

Bodhi, Bhikkhu (1998), 'Dhamma and Non-Duality'. Accessed at http://accesstoinsight.org/lib/authors/bodhi/bps-essay_27.html

Bodhi, Bhikkhu (2005), *In the Buddha's Words: An Anthology of Discourses from the Pali Canon* (Somerville, MA: Wisdom Publications)

Brach, Tara (2001), 'Awakening from the Trance of Unworthiness', *Inquiring Mind* vol.17:2. Accessed at https://inquiringmind.com/article/1702_20_brach_awakening-from-unworthiness

Brien, Kevin (2005), *Marx, Reason, and the Art of Freedom (2nd ed.)* (New York: Humanities Press)

Browning, Elizabeth Barrett ([1850] 2018), *Sonnets from the Portuguese* (London: Forgotten Books)

Buswell, Jr. Robert and Lopez, Jr. Donald (2014), *The Princeton Dictionary of Buddhism* (Princeton, NJ: Princeton University Press)

Camus, Albert ([1947] 2004), *The Plague, The Fall, Exile and the Kingdom, and Selected Essays* (New York: Alfred Knopf)

Cox, Laurence (2003), 'Liberation Buddhology'. Accessed at https://web.archive.org/web/20060811170445/http:/www.iol.ie/~mazzoldi/toolsforchange/buddhist/buddhology.html

Csíkszentmihályi, Mihály (2002), *Flow: The Classic Work on How to Achieve Happiness* (London: Rider)

Dawkins, Richard (2006), *The God Delusion* (New York: Bantam Books)

De Kadt, Katya (2023), 'The value of meditational awareness and Buddhist ethics for progressive groups', *Secular Buddhist Network*. Accessed at https://secularbuddhistnetwork.org/the-value-of-meditational-awareness-and-buddhist-ethics-for-progressive-groups

de Waal, Frans (2013), *The Bonobo and the Atheist: In Search of Humanism Among the Primates* (New York: W.W. Norton and Company)

Democratic Socialists of America (2017), 'DSA Guidelines for Respectful Discussion', *Democratic Socialists of America*. Accessed at https://dsausa.org/organize/respectful_discussion

Donoho, Travis (2021), 'Mindful in the Struggle: What Buddhism Brings to Socialism', *Religious Socialism*. Accessed at https://religioussocialism.org/mindful_in_the_struggle_what_buddhism_brings_to_socialism

Draper, Hal ([1968] 2019), 'The Two Souls of Socialism' in *Socialism from Below* (Chicago: Haymarket Books) 9–45

Edelglass, William and Jay Garfield (eds.) (2009), *Buddhist Philosophy: Essential Readings* (Oxford: Oxford University Press)

Foster, John (2022), *Capitalism in the Anthropocene: Ecological Ruin or Ecological*

References

Revolution (New York: Monthly Review Press)

Fraser, Nancy (2022), *Cannibal Capitalism: How Our System is Devouring Democracy, Care, and the Planet – And What to Do About It* (London: Verso)

Freire, Paulo and Horton, Myles Horton (1990), *We Make the Road by Walking: Conversations on Education and Social Change* (Philadelphia, PA: Temple University Press)

Fronsdal, Gil (Tr.) (2005), *The Dhammapada: A New Translation of the Buddhist Classic With Annotations* (Boston: Shambhala)

Garfield, Jay (2022), *Losing Ourselves: Learning to Live Without a Self* (Princeton, NJ: Princeton University Press)

Geras, Norman (1983), *Marx and Human Nature: Refutation of a Legend* (London: Verso)

Goldstein, Joseph (2003), *Insight Meditation: The Practice of Freedom* (Boston: Shambhala)

Gramsci, Antonio (1957), *The Modern Prince & Other Writings* (New York: International Publishers)

Hägglund, Martin (2019), *This Life: Secular Faith and Spiritual Freedom* (New York: Pantheon)

Harvey, Peter (2013), *An Introduction to Buddhism: Teachings, History and Practices.* 2nd ed. (Cambridge: Cambridge University Press)

Hick, John (1993), *God and the Universe of Faiths* (Oxford, England: Oneworld Publications)

Higgins, Winton (2020), 'Dharmic existentialist ethics in a time of pandemic', *Secular Buddhist Network.* Accessed at https://secularbuddhistnetwork.org/dharmic-existentialist-ethics-in-a-time-of-pandemic

Higgins, Winton (2021a), *Revamp: Writings on Secular Buddhism* (Wellington: Aotearoa New Zealand: Tuwhiri)

Higgins, Winton (2021b), 'Response to Mike Slott's 'Reexamining "truths" and "tasks" in secular Buddhism', *Secular Buddhist Network.* Accessed at https://secularbuddhistnetwork.org/response-to-mike-slotts-reexamining-truths-and-tasks-in-secular-buddhism

Holmes, Robyn (2020), *Cultural Psychology: Exploring Culture and Mind in Diverse Communities* 2nd ed. (London: Oxford University Press)

Ikeda, Mushim Patricia (2017), 'One Activist's Oath: First, Vow Not to Burn Out'. Accessed at https://mushimikeda.com/blog/2017/11/15/one-activists-oath-first-vow-not-to-burn-out

Iyer, Pico (2008), *The Open Road: The Global Journey of the Fourteenth Dalai Lama* (New York: Knopf)

James, C.L.R. and Lee, Grace C. with the collaboration of Castoriadis, Carlos, ([1958] 2006), *Facing Reality* (Chicago: Charles H. Kerr)

Jones, Ken (2003), *The New Social Face of Buddhism: An Alternative Sociopolitical Perspective* (Somerville, MA: Wisdom Publications)

King, Sallie (1997), 'Buddha-Nature Is Impeccably Buddhist', In *Pruning the Bodhi Tree: The Storm Over Critical Buddhism,* eds. Jamie Hubbard and Paul Swanson, 174–92, (Honolulu: University of Hawaii Press)

Kornfield, Jack (1993), *A Path With Heart: A Guide Through the Perils and Promises of Spiritual Life* (New York: Bantam Books)

Kotler, Arnold (ed.) (1996), *Engaged Buddhist Reader* (Berkeley, CA: Parallax Press)

Kramer, Gregory (2007), *Insight Dialogue: The Interpersonal Path to Freedom* (Boston: Shambhala)

Leopold, David (2020), 'Karl Marx and the Capabilities Approach', In Chiappero-Martinetti E, Osmani S, and Qizilbash M, eds. *The Cambridge Handbook of the Capability Approach* (Cambridge: Cambridge University Press)

Loy, David (2008), *Money, Sex, and Karma: Notes for a Buddhist Revolution* (Somerville, MA: Wisdom Publishing)

Loy, David (2013), 'Why Buddhism and the West Need Each Other: On the Interdependence of Personal and Social Transformation', *Journal of Buddhist Ethics* 20 401–21. Accessed at http://blogs.dickinson.edu/buddhistethics/2013/09/22/why-buddhism-and-the-west-need-each-other

Loy, David (2020), 'How to be an Ecosattva', *Lions Roar*. Accessed at https://lionsroar.com/how-to-be-an-ecosattva

Luxemburg, Rosa ([1915] 2004), 'The Junius Pamphlet', In Peter Hudis and Kevin B. Anderson (eds.) *The Rosa Luxemburg Reader* (New York: Monthly Review Press) pp. 312–41

Lyotard, Jean-Francois (1984), *The postmodern condition: A report on knowledge* (G. Bennington & B. Massumi, Trans.) (Minneapolis, MN: University of Minnesota Press)

Macpherson, C.B. (1962), *The Political Theory of Possessive Individualism* (London: Oxford University Press)

Magid, Barry (2002), *Ordinary Mind: Exploring the Common Ground of Zen and Psychotherapy* (Somerville, MA: Wisdom Publications)

References

Majjhima Nikāya. Satipaṭṭhāna Sutta (MN 10). Accessed at https://suttacentral.net/mn10/en/sujato?lang=en

Majjhima Nikāya. The Shorter Discourse to Mālunkyāputta (MN 63). Accessed at https://suttacentral.net/mn63/en/bodhi

Marx, Karl ([1845] 1972), 'Theses on Feuerbach', In Robert Tucker (ed) *The Marx-Engels Reader* (New York: W.W. Norton) pp. 108–09

Marx, Karl ([1846] 1972), 'The German Ideology: Part I', In Robert Tucker (ed), *The Marx-Engels Reader* (New York: W.W. Norton) pp. 110–64

Marx, Karl ([1848]1959), 'Manifesto of the Communist Party', In Lewis Feuer (ed), *Basic Writings on Politics and Philosophy: Karl Marx and Friedrich Engels* (New York: Anchor Books) pp. 1–41

Marx, Karl ([1867] 1976), *Capital, v 1.* (New York: Penguin Books)

Marx, Karl ([1871] 1972), 'The Civil War in France', In Robert Tucker (ed), The *Marx-Engels Reader* (New York: W.W. Norton) pp. 526–76

Marx, Karl (1880), 'The Programme of the Parti Ouvrier', *Marxist Internet Archive.* Accessed at https://marxists.org/archive/marx/works/1880/05/parti-ouvrier.htm

Maslow, Abraham ([1964] 1994), *Religions, Values, and Peak-Experiences* (New York: Penguin Books)

McLeod, Melvin (ed.) (2006), *Mindful Politics: A Buddhist Guide to Making the World a Better Place* (Somerville, MA: Wisdom Publishing)

McMahan, David (2008), *The Making of Buddhist Modernism* (London: Oxford University Press)

McMahan, David (2023), *Rethinking Meditation: Buddhist Meditative Practices in Ancient and Modern Worlds* (London: Oxford University Press)

Naito, Ryo et al (2023), 'Social isolation as a risk factor for all-cause mortality: Systematic review and meta-analysis of cohort studies', *PLoS One* 18 (1). Accessed at https://journals.plos.org/plosone/article?id=10.1371/journal.pone.0280308

Nhat Hanh, Thich (1993), *Love in Action: Writings on Nonviolent Social Change* (Berkeley, CA: Parallax Press)

Nhat Hanh, Thich (1994), 'The Next Buddha May Be a Sangha', *Inquiring Mind*. Accessed at https://www.inquiringmind.com/article/1002_41_thich-nhat-hanh

Nhat Hanh, Thich ([1987] 2020), *Interbeing: The 14 Mindfulness Trainings of Engaged Buddhism* (Berkeley, CA: Parallax Press)

Nussbaum. Martha (2003), 'Capabilities as Fundamental Entitlements: Sen and Social Justice', *Feminist Economics* 9 (2–3), pp. 33–59

One Earth Sangha (2014), 'The Earth as Witness: International Dharma Teachers' Statement on Climate Change', *One Earth Sangha*. Accessed at http://www.oneearthsangha.org/articles/earth-as-witness

Pinker, Steven (2011), *The Better Angels of Our Nature: Why Violence Has Declined*. (New York: Viking Press)

Priest, Graham (2022), *Capitalism – its Nature and its Replacement: Buddhist and Marxist Insights* (London: Routledge)

Purser, Ron (2019), *McMindfulness: how mindfulness became the new capitalist spirituality* (Marquette, MI: Repeater Press)

Queen, Christopher (ed.) (2000), *Engaged Buddhism in the West* (Somerville, MA: Wisdom Publishing)

Queen, Christopher and Sallie King (eds.) (1996), *Engaged Buddhism: Buddhist Liberation Movements in Asia* (Albany, NY: State University of New York Press)

Reeves, Gene (2001), 'Divinity in Process Thought and the Lotus Sutra', *Journal of Chinese Philosophy* vol. 28(4) pp. 357–69

Rosenberg, Marshall (2015), *Nonviolent Communication: A Language of Life* (Encintas, CA: PuddleDancer Press)

Saito, Kohei (2023), *Marx in the Anthropocene: Towards the Idea of Degrowth Communism*. (Cambridge: Cambridge University Press)

Salzberg, Sharon (2011), *Real Happiness: The Power of Meditation* (New York: Workman Press)

Samyutta Nikāya. Anuradha Sutta: To Anuradha. (SN 22.86). Accessed at https://www.accesstoinsight.org/tipitaka/sn/sn22/sn22.086.than.html

Sapolsky, Robert (2017), *Behave: The Biology of Humans at our Best and Worst* (New York: Penguin Books)

Secular Buddhist Network (2020), 'Stephen Batchelor on a "Secular Perspective on the Eightfold Path"', *Secular Buddhist Network*. Accessed at https://secularbuddhistnetwork.org/stephen-batchelor-on-a-secular-perspective-on-the-eightfold-path

Secular Buddhist Network (2022a), 'Stephen Batchelor on an ethics of uncertainty', *Secular Buddhist Network*. Accessed at https://secularbuddhistnetwork.org/stephen-batchelor-on-the-ethics-of-uncertainty

Secular Buddhist Network (2022b), 'Stephen Batchelor's program on Mindfulness Based Human Flourishing', *Secular Buddhist Network*. Accessed at https://

References

secularbuddhistnetwork.org/stephen-batchelors-program-on-mindfulness-based-human-flourishing

Segall, Seth Zuihō (2020), *Buddhism and Human Flourishing: A Modern Western Perspective.* (London and New York: Palgrave Macmillan)

Shackley, Paul (2001), 'Zen Marxism', *Contemporary Buddhism*, vol. 2 #2, pp. 169–76

Singer, Peter (2023), *Animal Liberation Now: The Definitive Classic Renewed* (New York: Harper Perennial)

Slott, Mike (2011), 'Can You Be a Buddhist and a Marxist?', *Contemporary Buddhism*, vol.12 #2, pp. 347–63

Slott, Mike (2015), 'Secular, Radically Engaged Buddhism: At the Crossroads of Individual and Social Transformation', *Contemporary Buddhism*, vol.16 #2, pp. 278–98

Slott, Mike (2018), 'Core elements of a secular and socially engaged Buddhism', *Secular Buddhist Network*. Accessed at https://secularbuddhistnetwork.org/core-elements-of-a-secular-and-socially-engaged-buddhism

Slott, Mike and de Kadt, Katya (2023), 'Right Livelihood at $17.3 Million a Year?', *Religious Socialism*. Accessed at https://www.religioussocialism.org/_right_livelihood_at_17_3_million_a_year

Slott, Mike, de Kadt, Katya, and Struhl, Karsten (2022), 'The core life tasks and beliefs for a radically engaged Buddhist', *Secular Buddhist Network*. Accessed at https://secularbuddhistnetwork.org/the-core-beliefs-and-life-tasks-for-a-radically-engaged-buddhist

Streeck, Wolfgang (2016), *How Will Capitalism End? Essays on a Failing System* (London: Verso)

Struhl, Karsten (2017), 'Buddhism and Marxism: Points of Intersection', *International Communication of Chinese Culture*, vol. 4(2), 103–16

Struhl, Karsten. 2023. 'Socially Engaged and Radically Engaged Buddhism'. *Secular Buddhist Network*. Accessed at https://secularbuddhistnetwork.org/socially-engaged-and-radically-engaged-buddhism

Surry, Janet and Shem, Samuel (2015), *The Buddha's Wife: The Path of Awakening Together* (New York: Atria Books)

Suzuki, DT ([1934] 1994), *An Introduction to Zen Buddhism* (New York: Grove Press)

Suzuki, Shunryu ([1970] 2020), *Zen Mind, Beginner's Mind* (Boston: Shambhala)

Thanissaro, Bhikkhu (Tr.) (1997), *Upaddha Sutta* in the Samyutta Nikaya – 45.2.

Accessed at http://accesstoinsight.org/tipitaka/sn/sn45/sn45.002.than.html

Thanissaro, Bhikkhu (2011), 'Selves & Not-self: The Buddhist Teaching on Anatta'. Accessed at http://accesstoinsight.org/lib/authors/thanissaro/selvesnotself.html

Thera, Ñāṇavīra ([1963]1987), *Clearing the Path* (Belgium: Path Press)

Watson, Bruce (2010), *Freedom Summer: The Savage Season of 1964 That Made Mississippi Burn and Made America a Democracy* (New York: Penguin)

Wright, Erik Olin (2021), *How to Be an Anti-capitalist in the 21st Century* (London: Verso)

Zizek, Slavoj (2001), 'From Western Marxism to Western Buddhism', *Cabinet* 2. Accessed at http://www.cabinetmagazine.org/issues/2/western.php

Notes

Preface

1 Freire and Horton 1990

Introduction

2 Slott and de Kadt 2023.

3 Thera [1963] 1987.

4 Slott, de Kadt, and Struhl 2022.

Chapter 1

5 This chapter is a substantially revised version of Slott 2011.

6 Brien 2005; Struhl 2017; and Priest 2022.

7 Cox 2003.

8 Jones 2003: 118.

9 Struhl 2017.

10 Pinker 2011.

11 Marx [1848] 1959: 37.

12 Marx [1846] 1972: 124.

13 Browning [1850] 2018.

14 Zizek 2001.

15 Kotler 1996; Queen 2000; and McLeod 2006.

16 Jones 2003: 222.

17 Geras 1993.

18 Marx [1846] 1972: 113.

19 Gramsci 1957.
20 Iyer 2009: 77.
21 Marx [1848] 1959: 29.

Chapter 2

22 This chapter is a substantially revised version of Slott 2015.
23 Shackley 2001.
24 Batchelor 1997, 2010, 2012, 2015, and 2017.
25 Queen and King 1996.
26 Loy 2013.
27 Batchelor 2015.
28 Dawkins 2006.
29 Batchelor 2010, 2012, and 2015.
30 Thera [1963] 1987.
31 Batchelor 2017: 81–100.
32 Batchelor 2015: 115–16.
33 Hick 1973.
34 Bodhi 1998.
35 Goldstein 2003: 83.
36 Bodhi 2005: 367–68.
37 Edelglass and Garfield 2009: 26–103; Harvey 2013: 114–50.
38 Suzuki 1934: 95.
39 I recognize that this view of Buddha Nature is strongly disputed by some. For example, Sallie King (1997) has argued that Buddha Nature does not entail any notion of an ultimate ground or primary substance, but '…is a soteriological device and is ontologically neutral' (p. 190). In addition, some have interpreted Buddha Nature as meaning that we have the seeds of enlightenment, which need to be cultivated in our life. This interpretation too does not depend on the existence of an ultimate reality.
40 Reeves 2001: 360.
41 Kornfield 1993: 211.
42 Sapolsky 2017.
43 Pinker 2011: 182.

Notes

44 de Waal 2013.
45 Fronsdal [tr.] 2005: 1.
46 Loy 2008.
47 Nhat Hanh 1993: 75.
48 One Earth Sangha 2014.
49 Marx [1845]1972: 108.
50 Marx [1867]1976: 283.
51 Marx [1871] 1972: 526–76.
52 Foster 2022; Saito 2023.
53 Watson 2010.
54 Struhl 2023.
55 Hägglund 2019: 5–7.
56 Thanissaro [tr.] 1997.
57 Kramer 2007.
58 Rosenberg 2015.

Chapter 3

59 Batchelor, Feldman, and Weber 2017.
60 Batchelor 2015: 149.
61 Batchelor 2015: 128-137.
62 Majjhima Nikāya 63.
63 Analayo 2021.
64 Higgins 2021b.
65 Analayo 2021.
66 Marx 1880.
67 Lyotard 1984.

Chapter 4

68 McMahan 2023.
69 Majjhima Nikaya (MN 10).
70 McMahan 2023: 15.

71 McMahan 2023: 8.
72 McMahan 2023: 52.
73 McMahan 2023: 55.
74 McMahan 2023: 172.
75 McMahan 2023: 135.
76 McMahan 2023: 212.
77 Purser 2019.
78 Batchelor 2015: 72.
79 Higgins 2021a: 25.
80 Maslow [1964] 1994.
81 Salzberg 2011: 49.
82 Magid 2002: 39.
83 Batchelor 2015: 232.
84 Batchelor and Batchelor 2019.

Chapter 5

85 Thanissaro 2011.
86 Samyutta Nikaya SN 22.86.
87 McMahan 2008.
88 Garfield 2022.
89 Garfield 2022: 34.
90 Garfield 2022: 42.
91 For example, Holmes 2020.
92 Macpherson 1962: 263.
93 Batchelor 2015: 200–01.
94 Thanissaro 2011.
95 Loy 2020.
96 Camus [1947] 2004.
97 Higgins 2020.
98 Camus [1947] 2004: 192–93.

Notes

99 Surrey and Shem 2015: xv.
100 Nhat Hanh 1994.

Chapter 6

101 Wright 2021.
102 Bhargava and Luce 2023: 6.
103 Draper [1968] 2019.
104 Donoho 2021.
105 Suzuki [1970] 2020.
106 Ikeda 2017.
107 de Kadt 2023.
108 Democratic Socialists of America 2017.
109 Luxemburg [1915] 2004.
110 Streeck 2016: 13.
111 Fraser 2022: xv–xvi.

Chapter 7

112 Batchelor 2015: 79–80.
113 Maslow [1964] 1994.
114 Csíkszentmihályi 2002.
115 Brach 2001.
116 Segall 2020: 66.
117 Aristotle 2011: 12–13.
118 Marx [1867] 1976: 283.
119 Leopold 2020: 44.
120 Marx [1846] 1972: 124.
121 Nussbaum 2003: 40.
122 Nussbaum 2003: 41–42.
123 Aṅguttara Nikāya 8.6.
124 Naito et al 2023.

125 Hick 1993: 133.
126 Hagglund 2019.
127 Singer 2023.

Chapter 8
128 Buswell and Lopez 2014: 1065-1102.
129 Batchelor 2017: 80.
130 Slott, de Kadt and Struhl 2022.
131 Secular Buddhist Network 2020, 2022b.
132 James, Lee, and Castoriadis [1958] 2006.
133 Nhat Hanh [1987] 2020.
134 Higgins 2021a: 94.
135 Secular Buddhist Network 2022a.
136 Hägglund 2022. 314.

Name Index

Aitken, Robert 24
Ambedkar, Bhimrao Ramji 104
Analayo, Bhikkhu 51, 56, 58, 59, 112
Aristotle xxiii, 131–35, 140, 144, 146, 170
Baker, Ella 105
Batchelor, Martine 86
Batchelor, Stephen xv, xxi, 23, 24, 49, 50, 51, 56, 58, 79, 86, 90, 98, 130, 147, 151, 152, 158, 162, 164, 165, 166, 177, 179
    reconstruction of the Four Noble Truths to the four tasks 26–28; 153–56
    truths and tasks 46–48; 50–54
Bhargava, Deepak 108
Bodhi, Bhikkhu 24, 28
Brach, Tara 130
Brien, Kevin 3
Browning, Elizabeth Barrett 10
Buddha (see Gotama)
Buswell, Jr. Robert 151
Camus, Albert 101–03
Chandrakirti 94
Cox, Laurence 4
Csíkszentmihályi, Mihály 130
Dalai Lama [Tenzin Gyatso] 21
Dawkins, Richard 25
De Kadt, Katya xix, xxiii, 119, 152, 180

de Waal, Frans   32
Democratic Socialists of America (DSA)   108, 110, 121
Donoho, Travis   117
Draper, Hal   109
East Bay Meditation Center   43
Edelglass, William   190 (Note 37)
Facing Reality   157
Feldman, Christina   47
Foster, John   38
Fraser, Nancy   124–25
Freire, Paulo   xvii
Fronsdal, Gil   191 (Note 45)
Gandhi, Mahatma   104
Garfield, Jay   94–98, 190 (Note 37)
Geras, Norman   15
Goldstein, Joseph   29, 30, 65
Gotama   xvi, xxi, xxiii, 10, 13, 15, 23, 24, 25, 32, 33, 40, 41, 42, 45, 46, 47, 56, 60, 61, 69, 72, 77, 79, 82, 90, 93, 103, 106, 143, 151, 152, 159, 170, 171, 173, 176, 177
    ethical and pragmatic teachings   26–28, 53, 54, 59
    view of not-self   29–31, 92, 94, 98, 99
    rejection of metaphysics   51–52
    interpretations of his teaching   57–59
Gramsci, Antonio   19
Hägglund, Martin   40–41, 147, 166
Harvey, Peter   190 (Note 37)
Hick, John   28, 146
Higgins, Winton   54, 80, 101, 161, 179
Holmes, Robyn   192 (Note 91)
Horton, Myles   xvii
Ikeda, Mushim Patricia   118
Insight Meditation   xv, xix, 29, 30, 65, 67, 84
Insight Meditation Community of Washington   43
Insight Meditation Society   65

Name Index

International Socialists (IS)   109–13
Iyer, Pico   190 (Note 20)
James, C.L.R.   157
Jones, Ken   5, 14
King, Sallie   190 (Note 39)
King, Jr., Martin Luther   104
Kornfield, Jack   xix, 30, 65
Kotler, Arnold   13
Kramer, Gregory   42
Lee, Grace C.   157
Leopold, David   136
Lopez, Jr. Donald   151
Loy, David   24, 34, 100
Luxemburg, Rosa   123
Luce, Stephanie   108
Lyotard, Jean-Francois   60
Macpherson, C.B.   98
Magid, Barry   85
Mahayana Buddhism   24, 29, 30, 56, 67, 89, 94, 100, 177
Mandela, Nelson   104
Marx, Karl   xxiii, 8, 9, 15, 16, 59, 112, 125, 132, 138, 140, 143, 145, 146, 170, 171, 172
    individual–society dialectic   36–39
    human flourishing   135–37
Maslow, Abraham   84, 130
McLeod, Melvin   14
McMahan, David   68–72, 94
Moses, Robert   105
Naito, Ryo   145
New American Movement (NAM)   xi, xii. 109
Nhat Hanh, Thich   35, 105, 106, 158
Niebuhr, Reinhold   161, 162
Nussbaum. Martha   xxiii, 80, 132, 137–38, 140–41, 143, 145–46, 148, 170

One Earth Sangha   35
Pinker, Steven   7, 31
Priest, Graham   3
Purser, Ron   73
Queen, Christopher   14
Reeves, Gene   190 (Note 40)
Rosenberg, Marshall   42
Saito, Kohei   38
Salzberg, Sharon   30, 84
Sapolsky, Robert   191 (Note 42)
Secular Buddhist Network   xvi, 155
Segall, Seth Zuihō   131
Shackley, Paul   23
Shantideva   94
Shem, Samuel   104
Singer, Peter   147
Streeck, Wolfgang   124
Struhl, Karsten   xxiii, 3, 7, 40, 152, 180
Surrey, Janet   104
Suzuki, DT   190 (Note 38)
Suzuki, Shunryu   117
Thanissaro, Bhikkhu   92, 99
Thera, Ñāṇavīra   xxi, 26
Tibetan Buddhism (Vajrayana Buddhism)   29, 67
Watson, Bruce   191 (Note 53)
Weber, Akincano Mark   47
Wright, Erik Olin   108
Zen Buddhism   24, 30, 67, 69
Žižek, Slavoj   12

www.ingramcontent.com/pod-product-compliance
Lightning Source LLC
Chambersburg PA
CBHW070620030426
42337CB00020B/3868